Happy, Healthy Children
a child care book

Written and illustrated by
Janie Hampton

MACMILLAN
PUBLISHERS

©Janie Hampton 1985

All rights reserved. No reproduction, copy or transmission
of this publication may be made without written permission.
No paragraph of this publication may be reproduced, copied
or transmitted save with written permission or in accordance
with the provisions of the Copyright Act 1956 (as amended).
Any person who does any unauthorised act in relation to
this publication may be liable to criminal prosecution
and civil claims for damages.

First published 1985

Published by *Macmillan Publishers Ltd*
London and Basingstoke
*Associated companies and representatives in Accra,
Auckland, Delhi, Dublin, Gaborone, Hamburg, Harare,
Hong Kong, Kuala Lumpur, Lagos, Manzini, Melbourne,
Mexico City, Nairobi, New York, Singapore, Tokyo*

ISBN 0 - 333 - 39030 - X

Printed in Hong Kong

Published in conjunction with Teaching Aids at Low Cost, PO Box 49,
St. Albans, Hertfordshire AL1 4AX

TALC received assistance in the production of this book as a low cost edition
from the Swedish International Development Authority.

To Pamella and Verily Vimbai Nyabadza
and Phillip Simbai Gwenjere of Zimbabwe.
May they grow into happy, healthy adults.

Many things can wait.
The child cannot.
Right now is the time her bones are being formed.
Her blood is being made.
And her senses are being developed.
To her we cannot say 'Tomorrow.'
Her name is 'Today'.

Gabriela Mistral of Chile.

Acknowledgements

The author and publishers wish to acknowledge, with thanks, the following photographic sources.
Church Missionary Society, pp 55 left; 120
Department of Information, Kenya, p 33
The Health Education Council, p 71
John and Penny Hubley, pp 3; 9; 16; 17; 42; 46; 48; 74
Rex Parry, p 14
UNICEF, p 10
WHO, pp 2; 4; 12 (photo J. Mohr); 23 left (photo J. Mohr); 24; 31 (photo P. Almasy); 47 right (photo Pierre Pittet); 55 right (photo P. Almasy); 96; 100 top (photo P. Pittet); 102 (photo J. Mohr).

The publishers have made every effort to trace the copyright holders, but if they have inadvertently overlooked any, they will be pleased to make the necessary arrangements at the first opportunity.

Foreword

by David Morley,
Professor of Tropical Child Health,
University of London.

I was very pleased to be able to respond when asked by Janie to write a preface for her book. Janie Hampton and her family have worked and played alongside their neighbours in a rural part of Africa, and her enormous respect for the mothers and what they can achieve comes out clearly in her book. She has practical experience of the health care of children in Africa, especially through her own children who have faced the same challenges as friends in their own village. Perhaps it is an advantage to her that she comes from an educational background, and has been able to absorb the essentials of health care and to show how such subjects as basic sex education and family planning can be passed on to parents.

Her approach reminds me of a study I saw a number of years ago in Cali, Colombia. I think her work has fulfilled the findings of this trial which attempted to dissect the priority needs of the child. In the study (see table, p. vi), malnourished children were drawn from slum areas and divided into three groups. Different resources were made available to each group. The three groups were compared to an 'elite' control group from a wealthy background. The group that received health care alone showed little change in growth or intelligence over the two years. This was in spite of the health care being comprehensive, including both curative and preventive measures. This health care was much better than that available to children in the slums from which they had come. The second group received good nutrition as well as health care. To ensure that the child was adequately fed they fed the whole family. This group caught up, in their growth, with the elite control group from the same city. The third and final group received health care, good nutrition and an intensly stimulating environment that was appropriate for children in that area. These children grew as well as the elite. In addition, owing to their stimulating environment, they caught up intellectually in 16 different tests of their social and intellectual development.

The priorities, then, for children must be first and foremost adequate nutrition. This means breast-feeding for at least one to two years and a weaning diet of high-energy food with enough protein. However, the children will be unable to take this diet unless they are protected against illness by immunisation, and treated for the diarrhoea and respiratory infections which are so common in childhood.

		RESOURCES MADE AVAILABLE TO CHILDREN			RESULTS
		Medical care	Adequate food	Stimulating environment	(after two years)
MALNOURISHED PRE-SCHOOL CHILDREN FROM SLUM AREAS	Group I	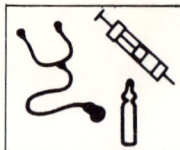			No change in growth or intellect
	Group II	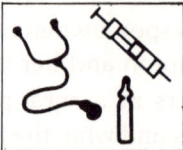			Growth as elite Little change in intellect
	Group III				Growth and intellect as elite
'ELITE'	Control group	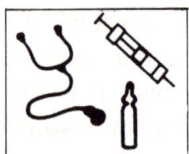			Full growth and intellectual development

At first, the average African child has an intensely stimulating environment and is in close skin contact with the mother or other members of the family. Unfortunately, for many, the appropriate environment lasts for just one or at the most two years. After this the child may not have the stimulation and experiences of the same-aged children in Europe and North America. All three priorities – adequate food, medical care and stimulating environment – interact to help the young child grow into a schoolchild who can start to understand better the complex world in which he or she is growing up. Moreover, these three priorities can be provided for all children, irrespective of the wealth of their family background.

In this book Janie has done much to show workers and mothers how they can help their young children to become happy, healthy children.

David Morley, FRCP

Introduction

This book is written as a resource book for primary, junior and secondary school teachers, secondary school students and student teachers, parents and adult literacy classes in Africa. It will also be useful for nurses and health care workers. It combines both simple English and important knowledge about the health care of children. It contains material which is relevant to all those who at any time have responsibility for the care of young children.

The book is written in simple English, as a second language. Long words have been used only where there is no alternative or where the word is worth learning, for example, 'immunisation'. The pronoun 'she' is used to stress the importance of girl babies and children as much as boy babies.

The health chapters are all based on prevention, rather than cure: there has been no attempt to explain how to mend a broken leg or cure pneumonia.

Chapter 2 explains reproduction in a warm, human way. It is not intended to encourage school children to experiment with sex.

The information and advice given is as appropriate as possible, bearing in mind that many readers will live in rural areas, without the availability of complicated equipment or services.

At the end of each chapter are questions and activities which have been directed at the children themselves. Some questions and activities are directed at younger children whilst others are more suitable for older children. Similarly there are passages which could be read by older children, or read to children of all ages by an adult. The questions and activities are only suggestions to give the teachers and students further ideas. The questions are designed to find out whether the pupils have understood the chapter. The answers can either be written down or be part of a class discussion. Some of the activities, such as drawing posters, can be done in the classroom. Other activities involve going out into the community and bringing information back to the school. Children will need some help from the parent or teacher to set up these activities.

Children learn what they live

If a child lives with criticism, he learns to condemn.
If a child lives with hostility, he learns to fight.
If a child lives with ridicule, he learns to be shy.
If a child lives with shame, he learns to feel guilty.
If a child lives with tolerance, he learns to be patient.
If a child lives with encouragement, he learns confidence.
If a child lives with praise, he learns to appreciate.
If a child lives with fairness, he learns justice.
If a child lives with approval, he learns to like himself.
If a child lives with acceptance and friendship, he learns to find love in the world.

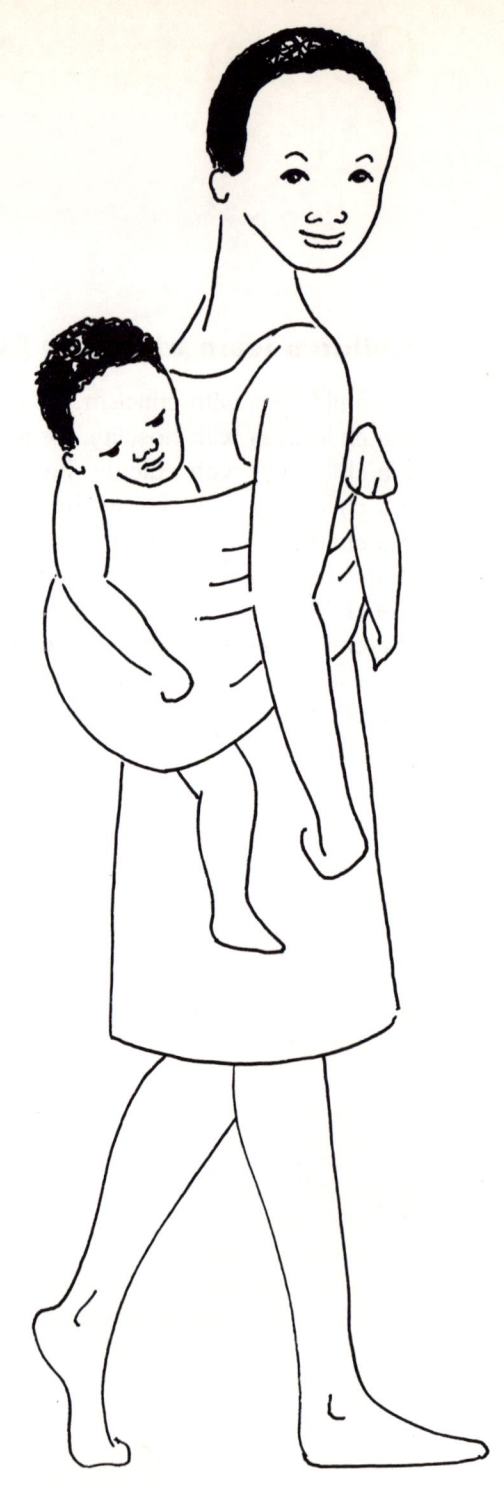

Contents

1 What is a happy, healthy child? 1
   Caring parents 1
   Good food and clean water 1

2 Where do people come from? 6
   Growing up 6
   Periods 7
   Conception 7
   Pregnancy 8
   Birth 12

3 New-born baby 14
   Security 14
   Sleeping 15
   Breast-feeding 16
   Bottle-feeding 19
   Clothes 21
   Bathing 22

4 What is a children's clinic? 23
   Immunisation 24

5 What should children eat? 28
   Energy food 29
   Growing food 31
   Protective food 32
   Non-foods 34
   Three-legged stool for healthy eating 34
   Introducing food to a baby 36
   Home-made baby foods 37
   Malnutrition 38
   Measuring strip 38
   Gardens 41

6 Why do we keep clean? 44
   Germs 44
   Animals and people 45

Flies	46
Rubbish	46
Clean water	47
Personal cleanliness	47
Teeth	48
Toothbrush	48
Public cleanliness	49
Drinking water	49
Latrines	50
Clean air	51
Rubbish	51
7 Sickness and health	**53**
Look with your eyes	53
Feel with your hands	53
Listen with your ears	53
Smell with your nose	53
Caring for the sick child	54
Diarrhoea	56
Special rehydration drink	57
Vomiting	58
Fevers	58
Colds and 'flu	59
Coughs	59
Pneumonia	60
Whooping cough	60
Mumps	61
Worms	61
Tapeworm Threadworm Hookworm	61-62
Roundworm Guineaworm	62
Paw-paw worm mixture	62
Skin problems	63
Scabies	63
Ringworm	63
Chickenpox	63
Ticks	63
Impetigo	64
Petroleum jelly rashes	64
Malaria	64
Bilharzia	65
Measles	66
Polio	66
Tetanus	66
Diptheria	67
Tuberculosis	68

8 Making our lives safer   69
  Accidents in the home   69
    Burns   69
    Poison   70
    Choking   72
    Electricity   72
  Accidents outside   73
    Snakes   73
    Dog bites   73
    Roads   73
    Walking   73
    Cycling   74
  Cuts and wounds   76
  Water   76
  Shock   77

9 Playing with children   79
  Playing with babies   80
  Pre-school playgroups   81
  Games and activities   81
    Shops   81
    Clinics   81
    Dolls   82
    How to make a rag doll and carrier   82
    Helping in the home   84
    Toys   84
    Clay   85
    Pictures   85
    Bottle tops   86
    Size and shape   86
    Balancing   87
    Water   88
    The Sun   88
    Balls   88
    Music   89
    Play area   89
    Climbing frame   90
    Happy healthy snakes and ladders   94

10 How should children progress?   96

11 What should children wear?   101
  How to make a dress, a nightdress   103
  and pyjamas or shorts   105
  Knitted jersey for a boy or girl   106

12 What is child spacing? 108
  Methods for child spacing 110
  Teenagers 112
  Sexually transmitted diseases 113
    Gonorrhoea 113
    Syphilis 113

13 Disabled children 115

14 Smoking, drinking and drugs 123
  Smoking 123
  Drinking 124
  Drugs 124
    Addiction 125
    Dagga 125
    Pep-pills 125
    LSD 125
    Opium 126
    Glue sniffing 126

Glossary: meanings of words 129

Bibliography 137

Index 139

1 What is a happy, healthy child?

Caring parents

Happy, healthy children come from happy, healthy homes. Caring, loving parents make happy, healthy children. Children learn by example. If the parents of a boy are lazy, dirty, rude and selfish they cannot expect their son to be different from them. Children learn to be kind, responsible, polite and caring by watching these things in their homes.

Good food and clean water

Children must be fed well and live in a clean home to be healthy. Most sickness does not have to happen. If we all EAT WELL, keep ourselves

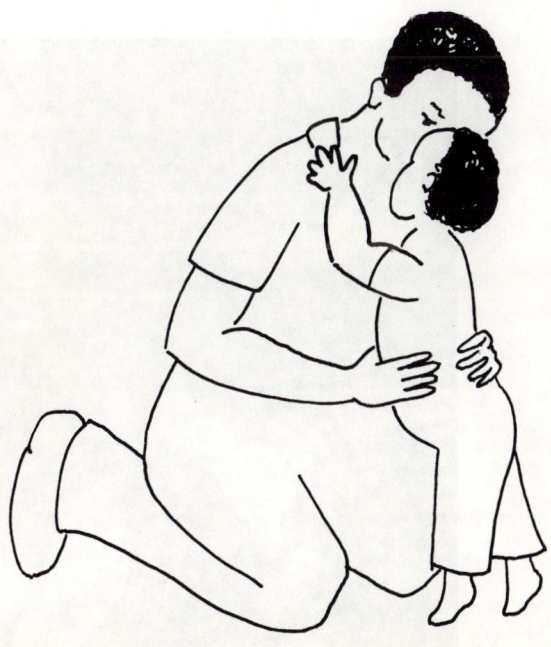

Children need love from fathers too

CLEAN, keep our homes CLEAN, then we can prevent most disease before it starts. If we go to clinics soon after illness is noticed then most diseases can be cured quickly. If all babies are immunised against diseases then they will be healthier.

Sleep is important in keeping children healthy and bright. Babies cry when they are tired. Children become cross and unhelpful. Many children cannot work well at school because they went to sleep too late the night before. The occassional late night will not do any harm, but if children get too little sleep for many nights in a row, they soon fall behind in school or become sick.

Everyone is different in the amount of sleep they need. They must learn how much sleep is enough for them, and not think it is 'babyish' to go to bed when feeling tired.

Love and security

Good health is not just in our bodies; it is also in our minds. Everyone, children and babies included, has feelings. We cannot see or feel other people's feelings. We only know if a child is sad or happy by the way she looks or acts. Small children show their feelings more than older children or adults. Small children cry loudly if they are unhappy but will soon laugh again if someone cheers them up. Older children have strong feelings too, but they may hide them.

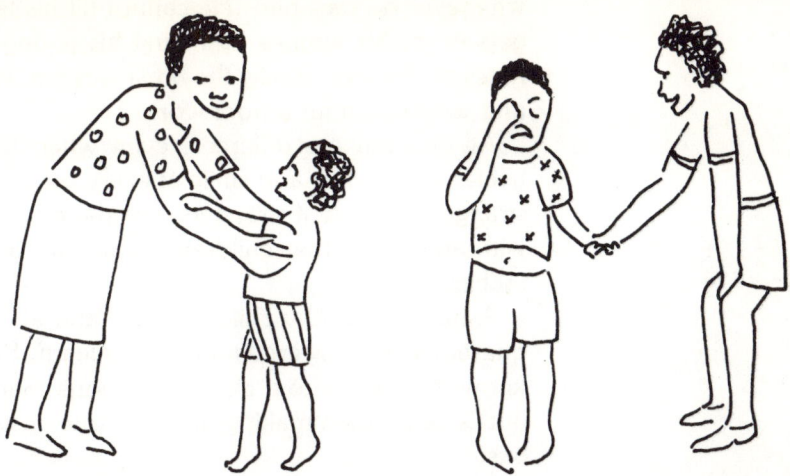

Every part of the day causes feelings. Children have many different feelings. Most of the time a child can understand his feelings. He knows that he is happy because he ate some delicious food, or that he is sad because his grandmother has died. Sometimes children do not know why they feel that way. A small child may cry because she is hungry. She was offered some food but she did not eat it. The reason she did not want it is because her mother has gone away for a few days. The child wants her mother so she will not eat. As soon as her mother returns she will be happy and eat again.

A boy may be finding school-work difficult. He is afraid to tell his parents that he may fail his exams. So he hits his younger brother

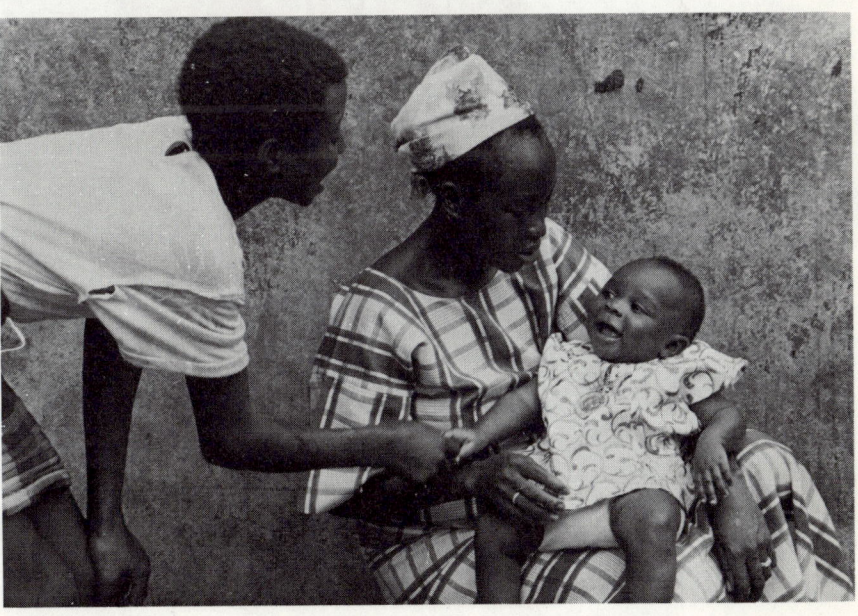

whenever he sees him. He cannot hit his teacher or his parents, so he gets rid of his worries by hitting his younger brother. It looks as if he hates his brother. Really the boy loves him very much but he is unhappy and worried about school-work.

All children are different, even when they are very young. Some babies are friendly and smile at everyone. Other babies are frightened of strangers and cry if strangers pick them up. Some children like playing with animals. Other children always run away from them, even small rabbits.

A happy, healthy child is bright and always asking questions. If the questions are answered then he will learn. Sometimes the adult may not know the answer to a child's questions. Saying 'I don't know, let's find out' is better than making-up an untrue answer or saying 'Go away, I'm busy'.

Happy, healthy children do not need to have rich parents. Some of the happiest and healthiest children come from poor families — but they do have plenty of love.

Children need lots of love and security. They need to know that whatever troubles they have, their parents will always be there to love and care for them.

Children need *love, good food*, a *clean home, security*, warm *clothes* and plenty of *sleep* to make them grow into good parents themselves.

Questions for pupils   1   What does a child need to be healthy?
2   Draw a picture of a happy, healthy family.
3   Is it good if a child asks lots of questions? Why?
4   Write a story about two children. One is happy and healthy and the other is sad and sick. What happens to them?

Activities for pupils   1   Talk about good and bad feelings with your class. What things make you feel angry, jealous, sad or proud?
2   Find a sad child. Make him happy.
3   Next time you feel sad or cross, try forcing a smile on your face. Smiling uses half as much energy as frowning. Sometimes making yourself smile will make you feel better — it will certainly make everyone around you feel happier!

2 Where do people come from?

Growing up

A person grows from a tiny egg into a full-sized baby inside a woman's **womb**. The womb is a special bag made of muscles inside a woman's belly. The womb is attached to the top of her **vagina** (see fig 1).

Small girls cannot have babies because their bodies are not yet ready. Between 10 and 14 years old a girl starts to grow breasts and hair under her arms and around her vagina. She also starts to bleed from her vagina for a fews days every month. This shows that she is turning into a woman and is now able to have a baby.

A boy cannot become a father until he also reaches **puberty**.

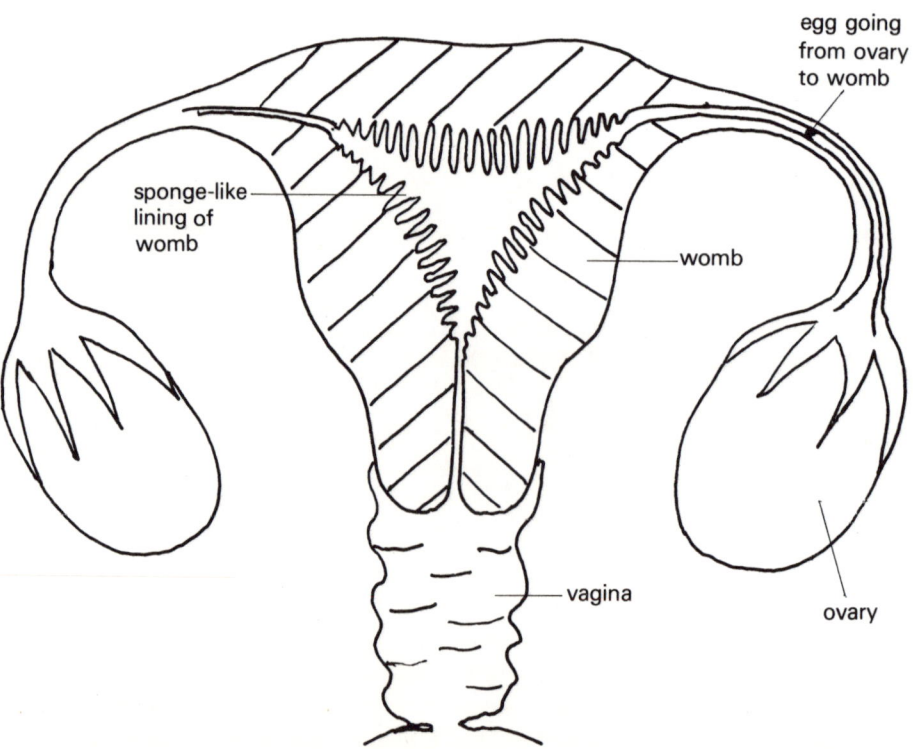

Fig 1 *Woman's reproductive organs: front view*

Between 12 and 16 years he will grow hairs on his face, under his arms and around his **penis**. His voice will become deeper and his body will grow stronger and more muscular.

Periods

Each month a new egg grows inside the woman's **ovary**. Every woman has two ovaries inside her belly. The ovaries take it in turns to produce one egg each month. This egg travels along a narrow tube from the ovary to the womb. The egg is so small that it takes about 5 days to reach the womb. The egg may be fertilised by a man's seed which is called **sperm**. If the egg is not fertilised then it dies. It will come out of the vagina with the monthly bleeding, which is called a **period**.

Each month the womb makes a thick, spongey lining ready for the fertilised egg to grow in. If the lining is not needed because the egg has not been fertilised, then it comes away with the egg in the form of blood. Periods are quite natural and painless. When a woman is bleeding she is not ill or unclean. She has to wear a cotton wool pad in her pants to catch the blood. She needs to change the pads three times a day and burn them. She can still run about and do her work.

Periods last from 4 to 6 days. During this time a woman bleeds about 6 spoonfuls of blood. If she loses a lot more blood then she should visit a clinic. She could become **anaemic**.

Some women and girls have an aching belly for a day during their period. The best cure is to take 2 painkilling tablets, such as aspirin. It also helps if she runs on the spot and touches her toes 20 times.

Periods stop when a woman is pregnant. When she is between 40 and 50 years old they stop for ever. After that she cannot have any more babies.

Conception

When a husband and wife are very much in love they feel desire for each other. They lie down together, kiss, and touch each other's bodies gently. The man's penis grows stiff and when she is ready, the woman's vagina becomes wet. The man puts his penis gently inside her vagina. The couple feels warm, loving and satisfied. Many millions of sperms come out of the man's penis in some white liquid called **semen**. Sperms are so small that we cannot see them with our eyes. Each one has a head and a long tail — like a tadpole. The sperms swim up inside the womb in search of an egg. The first sperm to meet an egg will **fertilise** it. The fertilised egg can now grow into a baby. Half of the baby's character will come from its father and half from its mother. From the moment of conception it is already either male or female.

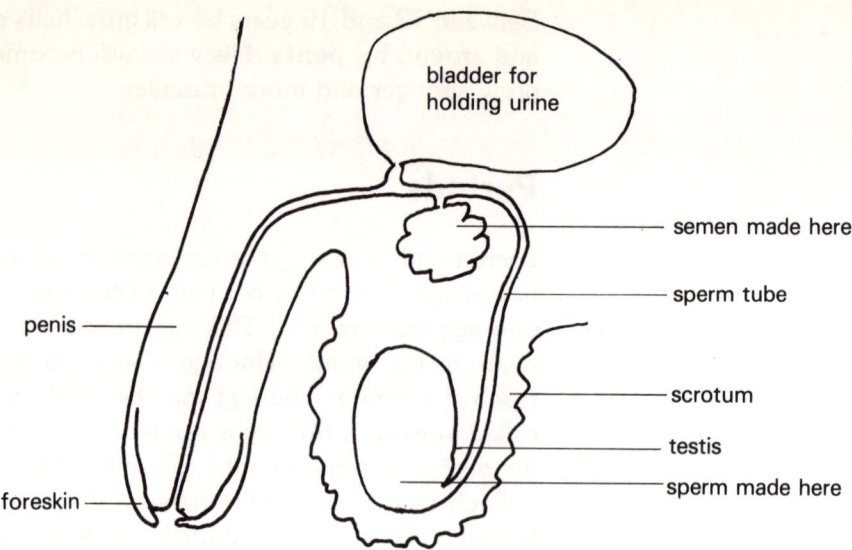

Fig 2 Man's reproductive organs: side view

The egg is made by the ovary, in the middle of the month between two periods. Making love at any time can make a woman pregnant, but it is more likely to happen in the days half way between two periods.

Pregnancy

The fertilised egg settles into the thick, spongey lining of the womb. As the egg grows the womb also grows bigger. A womb without a **foetus** is the size of a chicken's egg. After 6 weeks of pregnancy a womb is the size of an orange and the foetus already has a heart. By 8 weeks the foetus has all its fingers, toes and a face, but it is only 3 centimetres long. From then on it grows until it is big and strong enough to live in the outside world.

The foetus gets its food from a thick tube attached to the **navel**. The other end of this tube, or **umbilical cord**, is attached to the after-birth, or **placenta**, on the inside of the womb. All the food and oxygen that the foetus needs for its growth comes from the mother's blood through the placenta. The heart of the foetus pumps the blood along the umbilical cord. In the placenta the blood of the foetus picks up food and oxygen and then it returns along the umbilical cord to the foetus.

The placenta is also a filter. Many harmful things that are in the mother's blood are stopped from getting to the foetus; but some are not. If a pregnant woman smokes the foetus may not grow well.

Smoking and drinking are not good for either the mother or her baby. The babies of mothers who smoke are often smaller and weaker than

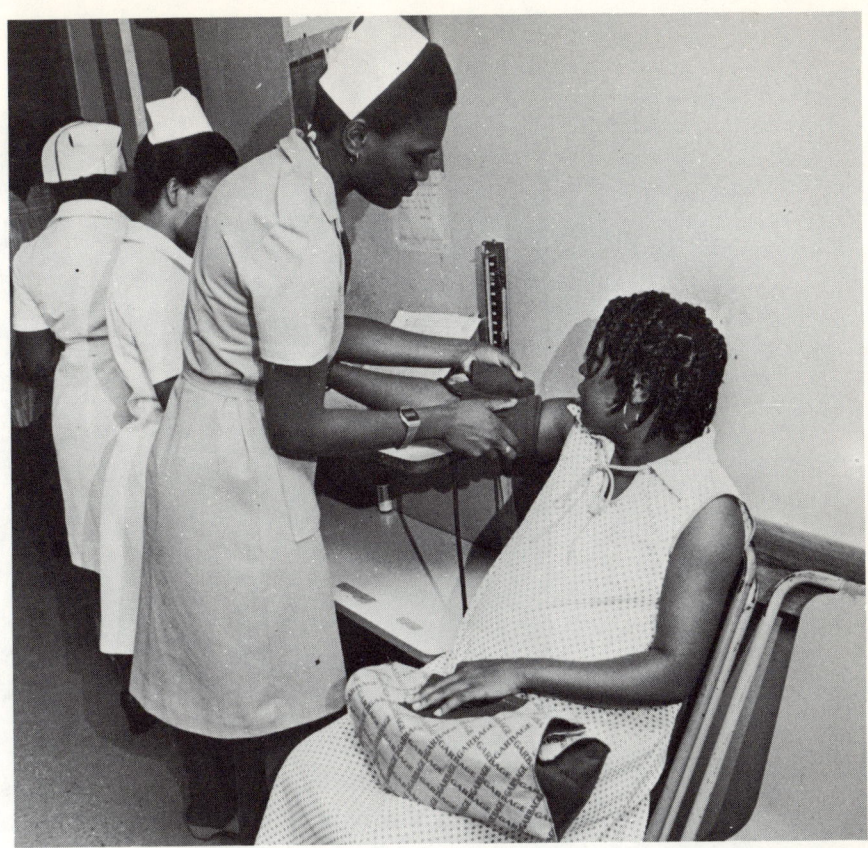

babies of non-smoking mothers. The poison in tobacco gets into the placenta. Pregnant mothers should not take any drugs or medicine unless the clinic has told them to. Some medicines can cause a foetus to be born **deformed** or even dead.

While the foetus is growing in the womb it is surround by a special watery liquid. This protects the foetus from any knocks the woman may have. It allows the foetus to move about easily. By 5 months the mother can feel her baby kicking and waving its arms. It can even turn right over.

When a woman is pregnant she must take good care of herself and the foetus growing inside her. She should go to her local **Ante-Natal Clinic**. There the nurse will ask her about any other babies she has had, and whether she has had any diseases. Pregnant mothers should have two injections during pregnany to protect their new-born babies against **tetanus**. The injections are given when the woman is 28 weeks and 32 weeks pregnant. The next time she is pregnant she needs only one injection.

The woman will be weighed and the nurse will feel her belly to see that the foetus is growing well. If there are twins inside her or if there are any problems, the nurse will advise the mother to have her baby in a

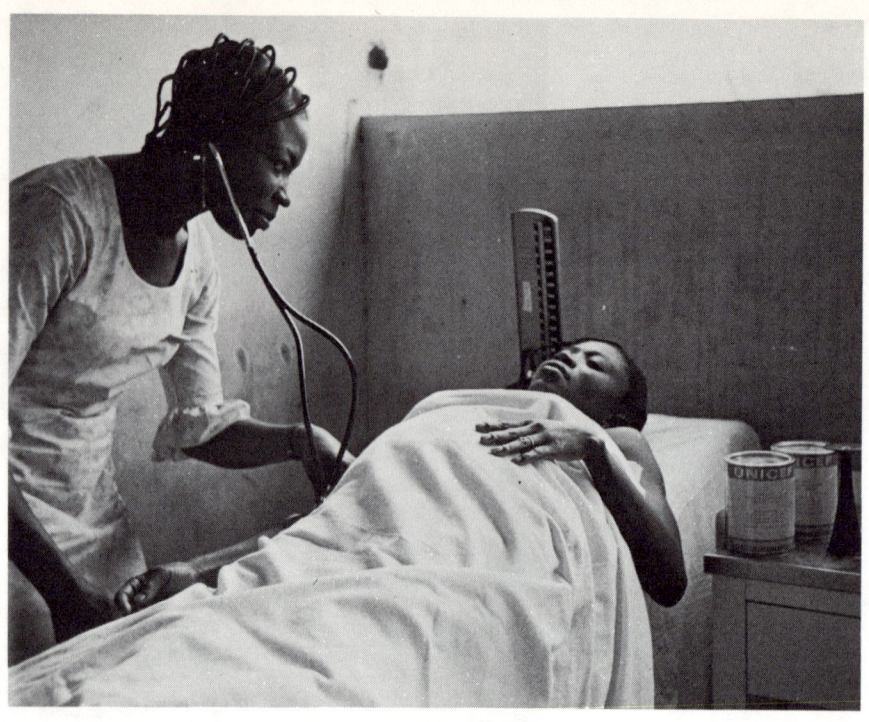

hospital or at the health centre. There are specially trained nurses to help and the right equipment to save a baby's life if anything goes wrong. Everything is kept very clean so there are no germs that a newborn baby might catch.

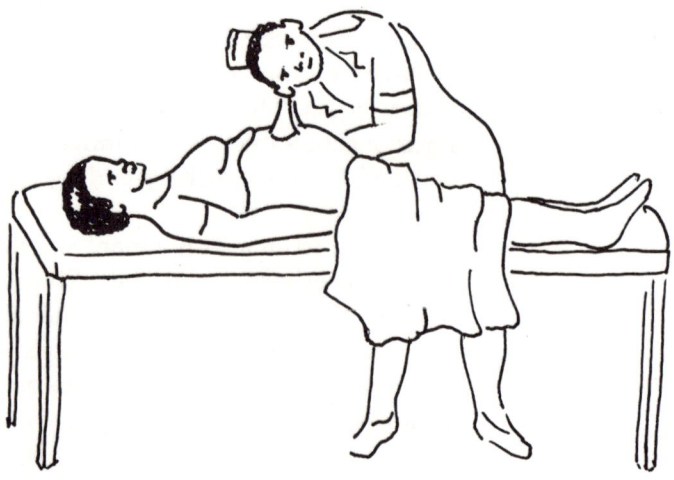

At the ante-natal clinic
Listening to the baby's heart inside the mother

The nurse at the ante-natal clinic may say it is safe to have the baby at home. The mother then chooses a **midwife** from her village or street. The midwife must be very clean. She must have helped at many births so she knows what to do.

Pregnant women need to eat extra well as they are feeding two people at once. They should eat lots of nuts (ground-nuts and tree nuts), beans, fresh fruit and vegetables and cereals such as sorghum, millet and wheat. As much egg, meat and fish as the family can afford should be eaten. Sweets and soft, fizzy drinks will make their teeth rot. The last weeks of pregnancy are important because this is when the baby's brain is growing. The mother must eat plenty of good food so she will have a big, strong baby.

Loose, cotton clothes are the most comfortable for pregnant women. Flat shoes or bare feet are easier for walking than high heels. A dress that unbuttons down the front will also be useful when she is feeding her baby.

When a women is pregnant her breasts grow bigger. This is so that they will be ready to make milk as soon as the baby is born. Mother's milk is especially made for babies and is much better than milk from the shops. A well-fitting bra will help to support her breasts and make her more comfortable.

Pregnant women get tired easily so they need plenty of sleep and rest. The whole family must help with the work – especially heavy jobs.

Rice, carrots, meat and paw-paw.

Milk curds, maize porridge, beans and cabbage.

Egg, spinach (amaranth), bread, nuts, milk and an apple.

Meals for pregnant mothers

Birth

At the end of 9 months the baby is ready to be born. The mother goes to the clinic or calls her midwife when she is in **labour**. She knows the baby is on its way when the womb begins to tighten up. The womb is a big muscle and it will help to squeeze the baby out. Sometimes the liquid that the baby is in starts to come out before the labour begins. Then the mother must rest until labour starts. Sometimes labour is painful, but if the mother walks about the house gently and keeps calm then it will hurt less.

First the opening at the bottom end of the womb will stretch and allow the baby's head to go into the vagina. The mother pushes hard and soon the whole baby will slip out of her vagina. The liquid in the womb will help the baby to come out smoothly. Most babies are born head-first but sometimes the feet come out first. The mother can be in a variety of positions when she gives birth. Some women like lying on their backs. Others prefer to squat, or sit up with someone holding them behind. Fathers can be very useful during the birth and enjoy the experience of seeing their child being born.

Birth usually takes from 2 to 24 hours. The first baby a woman has will take longer than later ones.

As soon as the baby is born she will start to breathe, and sometimes to

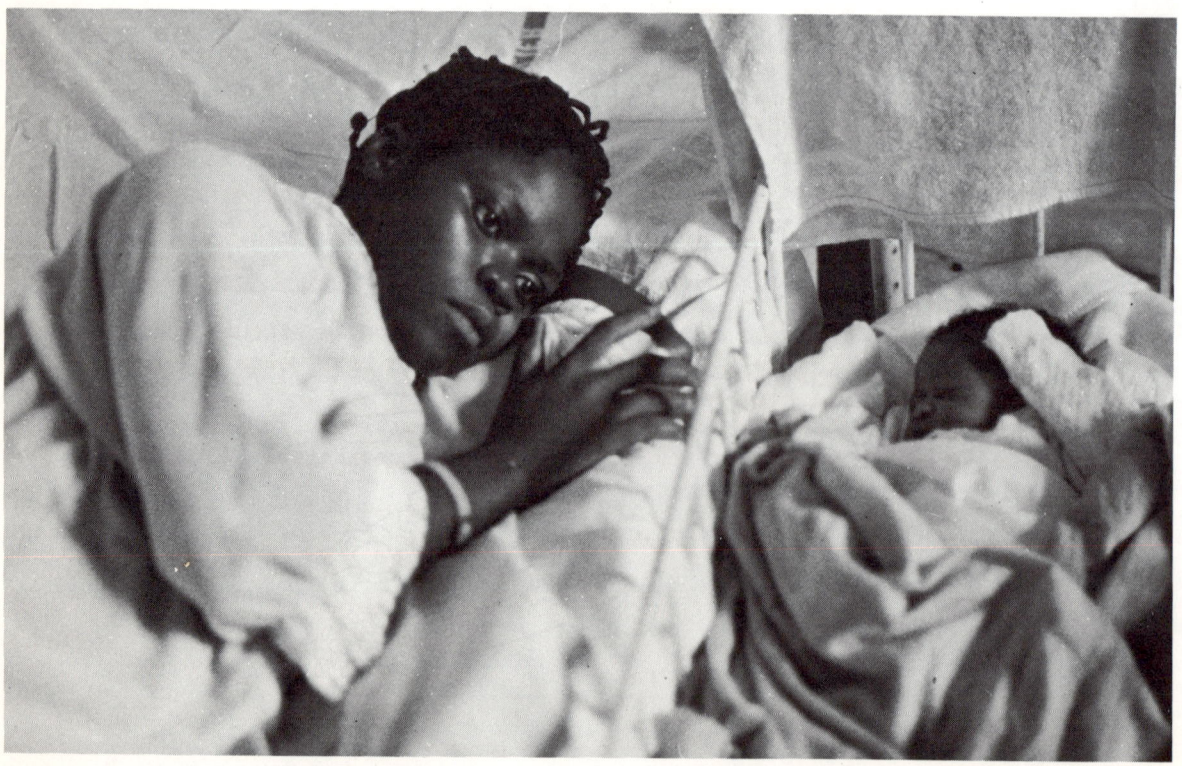

cry. The mother feels very happy to have her baby at last. The umbilical cord that is still attached to the baby's navel will be cut by the midwife and tied to stop it bleeding. This does not hurt the baby or the mother. The umbilical cord must be kept very clean and dry. If mud or other things are put on the umblical cord then the baby may become very ill with **tetanus**. After a few days the umblical cord dries up and drops off.

A few minutes after the birth, the mother pushes the placenta out. This has done its job so it is thrown away. Every baby has a new placenta. For about a week or two the mother will bleed a little, while her womb is shrinking back to its normal size.

The new-born baby is examined by the midwife to make sure that he is perfect. Then he is wrapped in clean, warm clothes. The mother holds the baby to her breast. A baby that is only a few minutes old knows how to suck milk.

After a few hours rest the mother can get up. But she has worked hard to have her baby. She should not return to normal work until she feels strong enough. She must have plenty of good food and rest, to keep her strong and to make milk for her baby.

Sometimes babies are born before 9 months of pregnancy. From about 7 months they can live, but they need special care in hospital with their mothers. Very small babies get cold quickly and they may have weak lungs.

Questions for pupils
1. What happens inside a womb?
2. Why do women bleed every month?
3. How many eggs does a woman make? How many seeds does a man make?
4. How does an egg become fertilised?
5. What is a placenta? What does it do?
6. What happens at an ante-natal clinic? Why should pregnant women go there?
7. What should pregnant women eat? Draw a poster of good food for pregnant women.

Activities for pupils
1. Copy the picture of a woman's insides. Name the parts without looking.
2. Copy the picture of a man's insides. Name the parts without looking.
3. Find out which day your local ante-natal clinic is held. Draw a poster telling mothers when and where the clinic is held.
4. Find out how many babies were born in your village or street last month. Were there more boys or girls? Were they all born at home?
5. Act a play with your friends about pregnant women. Some of you go to the ante-natal clinic. Others think it is a waste of time. What happens?

3 New-born Baby

A new-born baby weighs about 3.5 kg and is about 45 cm long. The baby has everything a person needs – fingers, eyes, ears, waving arms and legs and a loud voice – but she does not know how to use them yet. During the next four years she will learn how to walk, use a toilet, speak, hold a pencil and eat without making a mess.

A new-born baby needs love, food, cleanliness and clothes. Only the clothes need to be bought. Her parents can give her everything else.

Security

A baby needs lots of love and cuddling. She will grow quicker and be healthier if she feels that her parents care for her. An ill baby will recover more quickly if her mother is near her. Carrying a baby on the back is good. The baby will not feel lonely and is kept warm. The movement of her mother will help her to sleep and when she wakes up there is plenty

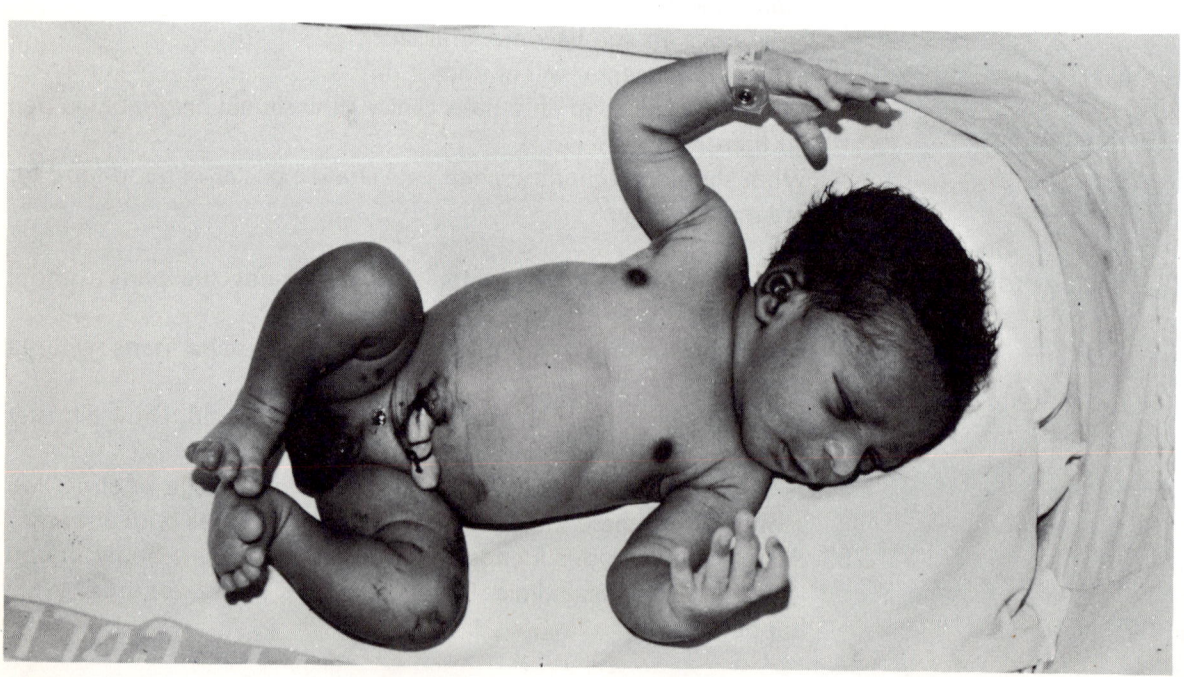

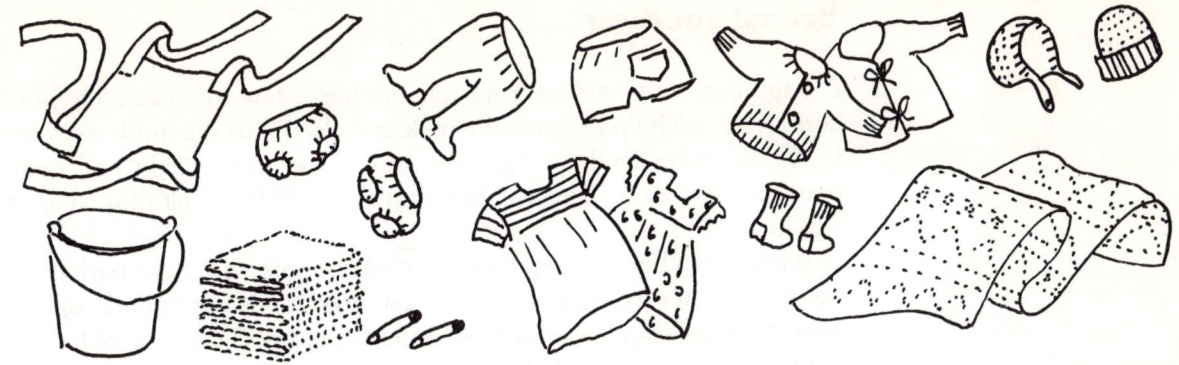

Things a baby needs

to see around her. Unless a baby is hungry or wet, she will rarely cry on her mother's back. Babies left on their own cry more than babies that stay among people.

Sleeping

A new-born baby sleeps most of the time, usually for 3 to 4 hours at a time. When she wakes up she will want to be fed. Babies have small stomachs, so they need feeding throughout the day and night. Big babies can last for up to 4 hours, but all babies are different. The important thing is to feed a baby when she is hungry and not to leave her to cry. Some babies learn to sleep all through the night when they are a few weeks old. Others are still waking in the night at one year. Do not worry about it.

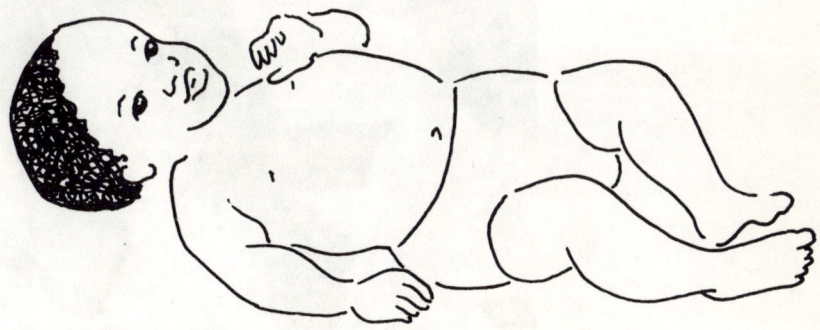

Healthy baby: shining hair and skin;
firm, plump arms and legs;
good appetite;
watches everything around her;
sleeps well.

Breast-feeding

A baby can start feeding from her mother a few minutes after she is born. This will help to make the milk and also helps the mother's womb to shrink. After feeding, the baby should be held upright and gently patted on the back. This will bring up any bubbles of air that baby has swallowed.

While a mother is breast-feeding often, she may not have periods. As her baby grows bigger and starts to eat other foods her periods will start again. Babies should be breast-fed until they are 2 years or older. The longer a baby is breast-fed, the better it is for her.

Breast milk contains **anti-bodies** which help to fight off any diseases that the baby may meet. This is especially important for very young babies who are not strong enough to fight diseases. A baby can get sick very easily. Do not allow any person who has a cough or 'flu to go near a new baby. If the baby has a fever, or her umbilical cord starts to bleed or has **pus** in it, take her to the clinic.

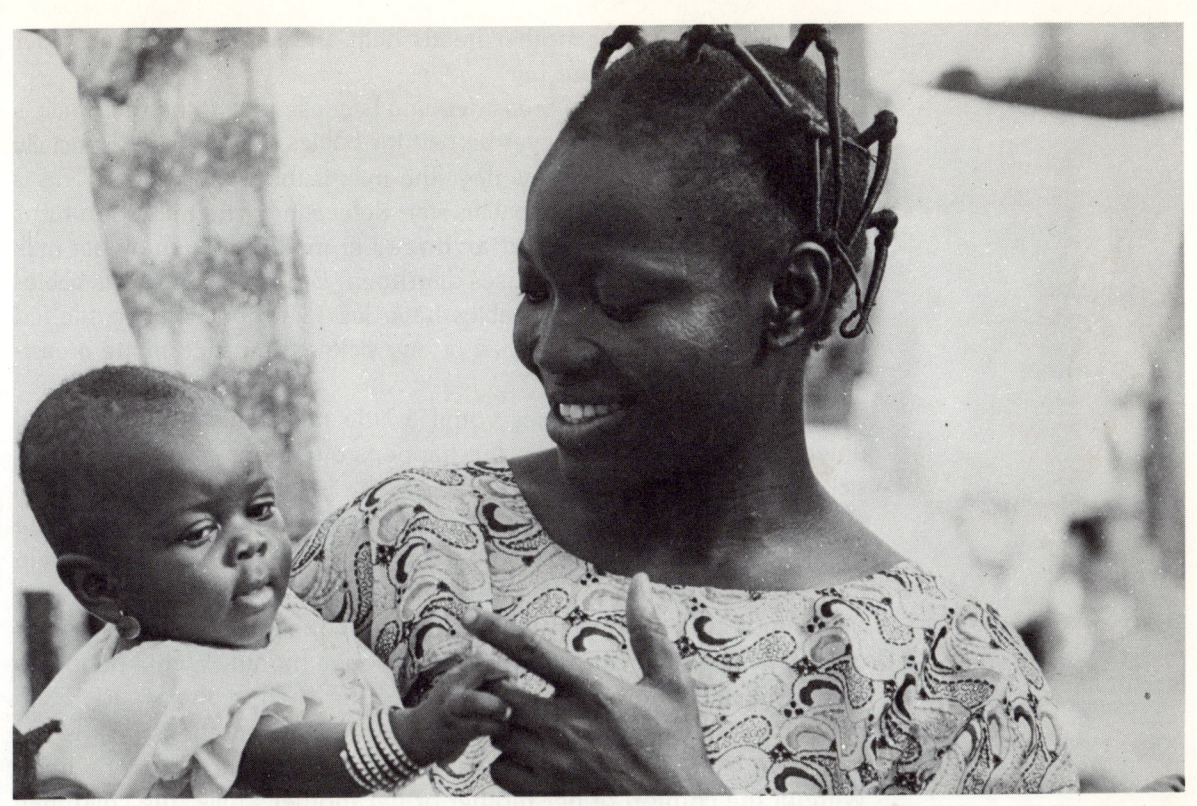

Many mothers think that breast-feeding is old-fashioned. They want to look modern by feeding with a bottle and powdered milk. This is because the companies who make the bottles and powdered milk want mothers to buy them. They put up pictures of fat babies next to their names. They hope mothers will think that bottle-feeding is better for babies. They just want mother's precious money. Dried or tinned milk is made from cow's milk. It is good for baby cattle but not as good for baby people. Breast-fed babies are healthier and happier.

Some mothers think 'I cannot make enough milk'. All mothers can make milk. Every time the baby sucks, more milk is produced. So the more often a baby sucks, the more milk will be made.

The mother needs to drink lots of water or other drinks. If she notices she has not been to the toilet all day, then she is not drinking enough. She must eat well too. Breast-feeding mothers should eat even better than pregnant mothers. Eating more food is easier and cheaper than buying bottles and powdered milk. There are no 'bad' foods for breast-feeding mothers. Milk, eggs, cheese, tree nuts, ground-nuts, meat, fruit, leafy green vegetables and cereals such as millet, sorghum and wheat will all help to make good milk. Vegetables cooked in oil are good. Sweets and soft, fizzy drinks are not so good – they are a waste of money.

Sometimes a young mother needs help and support from an older mother who can reassure her.

Some mothers give up breast-feeding because they think their milk is 'bad'. Mothers milk can never be bad for babies — it is made especially for them. During the first few days the milk is thick and yellow. This is especially to help new-born babies start defecating. The milk soon turns thin and white. If a baby has **diarrhoea** her mother may think her milk is 'bad'. Breast-milk never causes diarrhoea. Breast-milk protects babies from diarrhoea. Breast-fed babies have less diarrhoea than bottle-fed babies. All babies with diarrhoea or any sickness must continue breast-feeding.

After feeding, some babies vomit a little milk. This is quite normal unless there is a lot of vomit. If it happens often then the baby may be sick. Always take a baby to the clinic if she is sick.

Sometimes a new born baby's eyes turn yellow and she is sleepy. The mother should take care to feed her often. She needs lots of milk to help the **jaundice** go away and should visit the clinic.

If a mother becomes pregnant she can continue breast-feeding her child. She should give up slowly, over about a month. With 3 people to feed — herself, the baby inside her and the child at the breast — she needs to eat even more than before. A pregnant mother's milk is not bad. Sending the child to her grandmother's home does not help. Without the comfort of her mother or her mother's milk, the child may stop eating and become **malnourished**.

Mothers of twins can breast-feed them. Twins are usually small at birth

Breast-feeding twins

All you need to breast-feed!

so will need feeding more often. They may need other food earlier than a single baby would – before 4 months. Looking after twins is hard work, especially if there are other children in the family. Mothers of twins need all the rest and help the family can give them.

The breasts may sometimes become swollen and hot. The mother should not stop feeding her baby, that would make it worse. Cold, wet cloths put on her breasts will help. If she has a fever she could take aspirin tablets and visit the clinic.

Bottle-feeding

Lots of time

A bottle-fed baby will get diarrhoea more easily than a breast-fed baby. This is because breast-milk contains anti-bodies which prevent diarrhoea. It is also because it is difficult to keep the bottle and milk clean. Keeping a bottle **germ-free** needs a lot of *time, fuel* and *water*. Buying powdered milk and bottle and teats needs a lot of *money*. How many mothers have any time, fuel and money to spare? The only safe place to bottle-feed a baby is where there is plenty of clean water, electricity for boiling the water and bottles, no flies, plenty of kitchen tools like bottle brushes, cooking pans, detergents, spare teats and bottles, lots of time and plenty of money. If there are all these things then it is safe to bottle feed a baby, but it is not as good for any baby as breast-feeding.

If a baby could not be breast-fed she would need 27 kg of powdered milk in her first year. This can cost as much as a year's wages. If the powdered milk is not mixed properly the baby will quickly become sick. Many babies die because their mothers cannot afford to put enough powdered milk in their babies' bottles, so they become malnourished. Babies who are malnourished have diarrhoea. The diarrhoea makes them more malnourished. Babies with diarrhoea often die.

Lots of money to buy...

...lots of water...

...lots of fuel...    ...lots of bottles and teats...    ...lots of milk...    ...and lots of pans and jugs.

Things needed for bottle-feeding

If the mother dies, or is so ill that she cannot breast-feed, then the baby should not be given milk from a bottle. The only safe way to give a baby cow's milk is with a *cup* and *spoon*. A cup and spoon are easier to keep clean, and can be found in all homes. The cup and spoon must be put in boiling water to kill all the germs. The water must be boiled and then kept covered. The powdered milk must be measured very carefully and mixed with the correct amount of boiled water. Every feed must be freshly-mixed. Never keep the milk for the next feed because germs grow very fast in it. If the baby does not finish all the milk, it can be given to another child in the family. A baby needs at least 5 or more feeds a day.

At first the baby can only drink slowly from the spoon. She will soon learn how to drink from the cup. If she wants something to suck, then she always has her thumb!

If a mother dies then the baby's grandmother or aunt may take care of her and breast-feed her. Breast-feeding someone else's baby will not harm the baby or the woman. If the baby sucks on the breast every 3 or 4 hours the milk will start to come. Some special medicine will also help to make the milk.

Babies over 6 months may be given fresh cow's milk. It must always be boiled first.

If there is no breast-milk, use a cup and spoon, not a bottle

Breast is best

1 Breast-milk is made for human babies. Powdered milk is made for baby cattle.
2 Breast-milk is not too hot and not too cold.
3 Breast-milk is always clean, with no germs in it.
4 Breast-milk is always ready to drink, with no preparation.
5 Breast-milk does not go bad.
6 Breast-milk helps prevent diseases in a baby.
7 Breast-milk is free – no need to buy bottles and powdered milk.
8 Breast-feeding is warm and cosy for mother and baby.
9 Breast-feeding helps to space children.
10 Breast-feeding saves time.

Clothes

The most comfortable clothes for babies are made of cotton. Cotton washes easily and absorbs sweat and **urine** better than other fabrics. Clothes needed are towelling napkins (as many as the parents can afford), plastic pants, knitted or crocheted blanket, dresses and knitted jerseys, cotton vests and a hat and socks for cold days. A baby carrier and a bucket for dirty napkins are also needed.

Put the wet or dirty napkins in a bucket of water with a little washing powder. Wash them every day and boil them every few days. Dry them in the sunshine. The sun kills germs. Do not use bleach on them. Bleach makes the baby's bottom sore and the napkins wear out quicker.

If a baby's napkins are not changed at least 4 times a day then her bottom will get sore. If baby's bottom does become sore then it will get better if the napkin is left off as much as possible during the day. Wash

Sunshine kills germs in napkins and clothes

the baby's bottom with soap and water every time her napkin is changed.

Baby's first faeces are thick, dark, sticky paste. This is what was inside the baby before she was born. After a few days a breast-fed baby's faeces are soft and orange and do not smell. When food or cow's milk is given to a baby her faeces will smell. If a baby has liquid faeces, or diarrhoea, she should be given **Special Rehydration Drink** (see p.57) between feeds.

Bathing

All babies enjoy bathing. Any bowl or sink that is big enough will do. Make sure it is clean. Bath baby in a warm place, using a clean towel to dry her. Small babies get cold very quickly. Test the temperature of the water before putting the baby in. The water should be a little warmer than our bodies. Hold the baby's head with your arm and let her kick and splash. Be careful not to drop her — soapy babies are very slippery! Baby's first bath should wait until her umbilical cord has fallen off her belly. If it is pulled off it will bleed. Germs may enter the baby through her navel and make her very sick.

Questions for pupils
1. What can a new-born baby do? What does a new-born baby need?
2. Why is cotton the best fabric for babies? Draw a set of clothes for a baby.
3. How should napkins be washed? Help a mother wash the napkins.
4. Describe, in words and pictures, how to bath a baby. Help to bath a baby.
5. What should a breast-feeding mother eat? Draw a picture of the food.
6. For how long should a mother breast-feed her baby?
7. Why is breast-milk the best food we can give a baby?
8. Can twins be breast-fed? Draw a picture of twins breast-feeding.
9. Is it a good idea to send a child to her grandmother when a new baby is born?
10. Imagine you are a new-born baby. Describe your day.
11. With words and pictures show how to make a cup-and-spoon feed.

Activities for pupils
1. What do you need to bottle feed a baby? Find out how much 27 kg of powdered milk, 4 bottles and 10 teats costs at your local store.
2. Draw a poster about breast-feeding. Stick it on a wall in your village or clinic.

4 What is a Children's Clinic?

The Children's Clinic is held to prevent babies and children from becoming sick. When a baby is young the mother may need advice on feeding, clothing and caring for her baby. Even a mother of many children should take her baby to the clinic every month until she is over a year, and then every few months until she is five years old. The nurse may notice that the child is sick before the mother does.

What happens at the Children's Clinic?

The baby is weighed at each visit. This is to make sure that she is growing well. Each baby is given a special card called '**The Road to Health**'. This shows the weight of the baby on it. If the line goes *up* as the baby gets older, then the baby is growing well. If the line goes *down*, or falls below the green line printed on the card, then the baby is not eating enough or she is sick. If she is small for her age, then she is in danger of becoming sick. The nurse at the clinic can see on the card if the mother needs help and advice on how to feed her child. The Road to Health card is kept by the mother. She should take it with her whenever she visits the clinic or a hospital with her baby. The nurse will also write on it if the baby is ill, and when her **immunisations** are due.

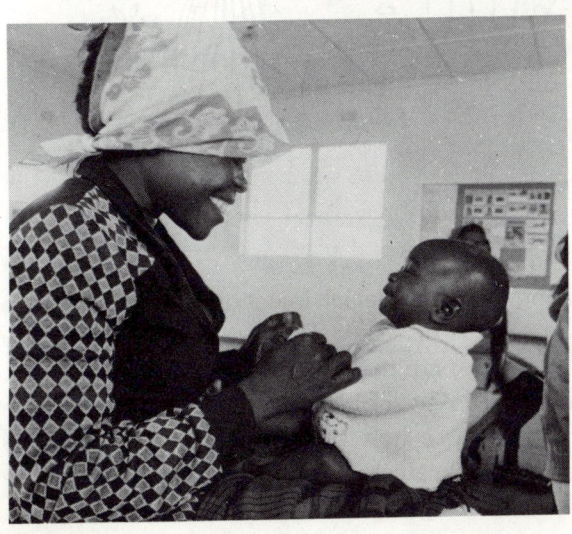
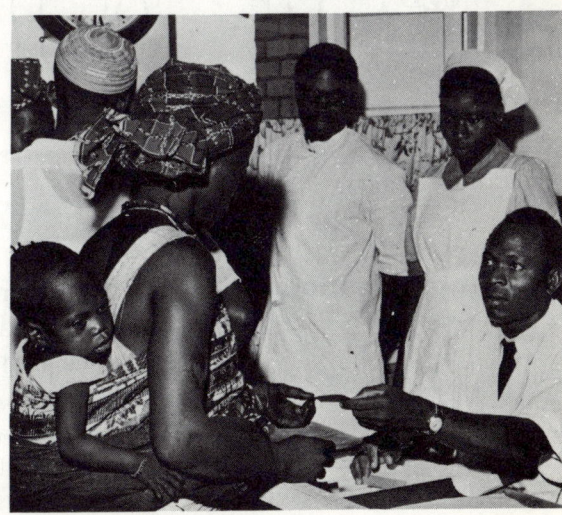

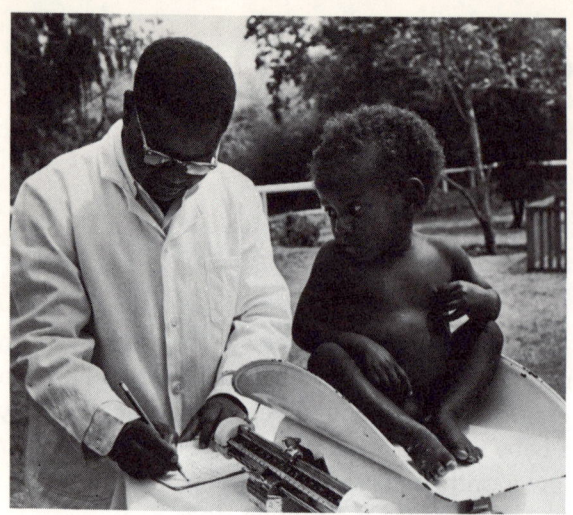
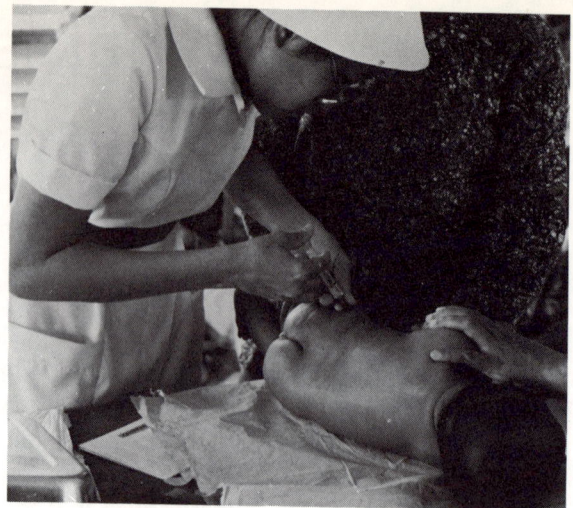

Children's Clinic

Immunisation   Immunisation means giving a baby special injections or medicine to prevent her from catching serious diseases. The six diseases that every baby should be immunised against are **measles**, **diphtheria**, **tetanus**, **whooping cough, tuberculosis** (TB) and **polio**. Any of these diseases can kill a child, or disable her for life. But with only a few immunisations all children can be protected for life. The clinic will advise each mother when she should bring her children in for immunisation.

Disease	Age	Method of immunisation
Tuberculosis (TB)	Birth and 5 years	Injection (BCG)
Diptheria Whooping cough Tetanus	3, 4 AND 5 months	Injection
Polio	3, 4 AND 5 months	Drops by mouth
Diptheria Tetanus	5 years	Injection
Measles	9 months	Injection

Fig 3   Ages for Immunisation

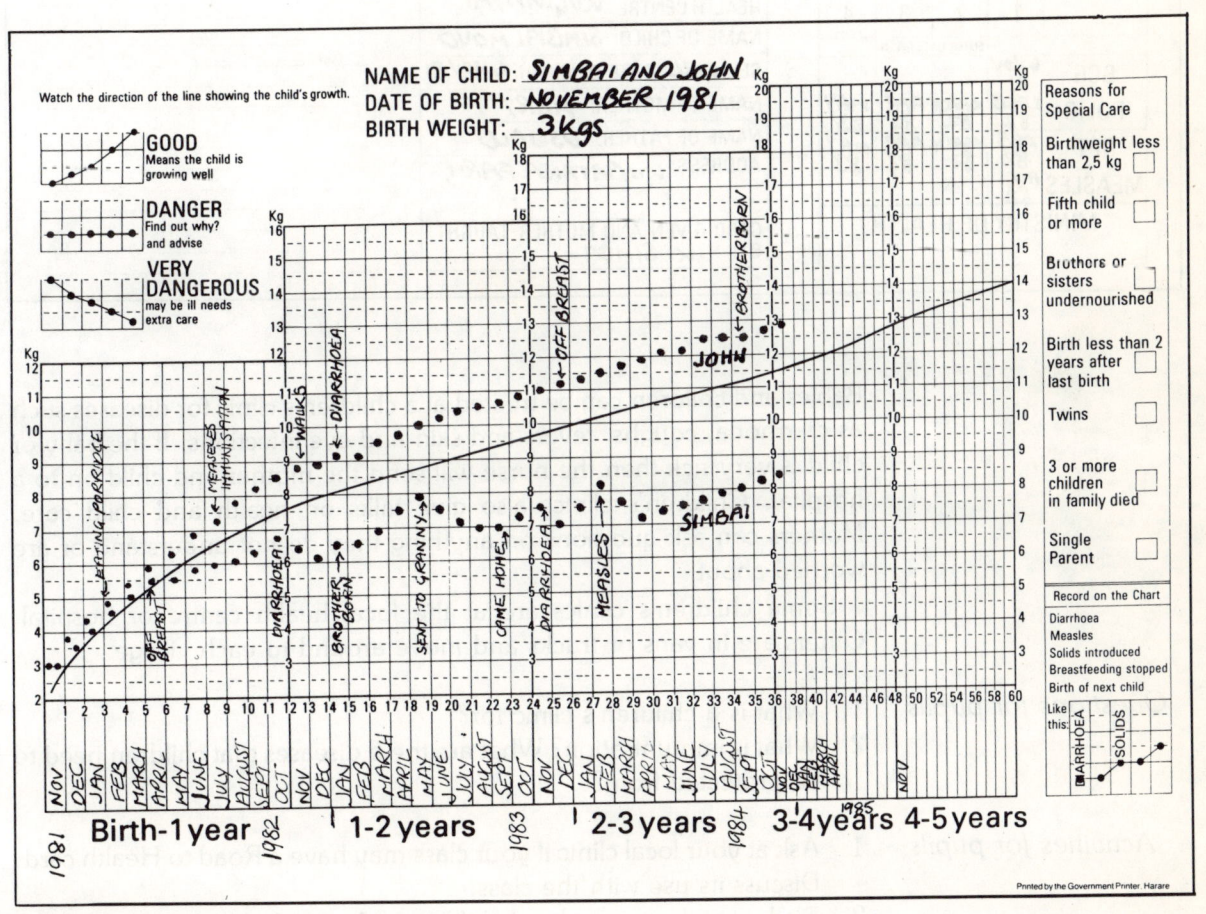

This 'Road to Health' card shows the progress of two children: Simbai and John. Which child is healthier?

IMMUNISATIONS
SCHEDULE:

AGE	IMMUNISATION
BIRTH	BCG
3 MONTHS	DPT 1 Polio 1
4 MONTHS	DPT 2 Polio 2
5 MONTHS	DPT 3 Polio 3
9 MONTHS	MEASLES
18 MONTHS	DPT and POLIO BOOSTER

DPT DIPTHERIA PERTUSSIS (WHOOPING COUGH) AND TETANUS

	DOSE 1	2	3	4
	ENTER DATE GIVEN			
BCG	6 NOV 81			
POLIO	7 FEB 82	MARCH 82	APR 82	MAY 83
DPT	FEB 82	MARCH 82	APR 82	MAY 83
MEASLES	AUG 82			

MINISTRY OF HEALTH

Child Health Card

Breast Feed for at Least 18 months

NAME OF HEALTH CENTRE: KUGWINYAI
NAME OF CHILD: SIMBAI MOVO
SEX: GIRL DATE OF BIRTH: 6 NOV 81
NAME OF MOTHER: MARY
NAME OF FATHER: OSWALD
ADDRESS: KUBATANA FARM,
CARD GIVEN AND MOTHER TAUGHT BY: K. SIMBA

Date of next visit	Symptoms	Treatment
JAN 83	Diarrhoea	Special Drink recipe taught to mother

Babies and children can be treated at a children's clinic for diseases such as diarrhoea, coughs, fevers and skin and eye infections. If the baby or child is very sick then the nurse will send the mother and child on to a hospital. Children's clinics also give talks on health and child care. Mothers can ask questions on anything they do not understand or are worried about.

Some children's clinics are at the local health centre or hospital. Others are in vans or trucks and move around to each village.

Questions for pupils
1. What is a children's clinic for?
2. What is immunisation? What are the 6 diseases that children need to be protected from?

Activities for pupils
1. Ask at your local clinic if your class may have a Road to Health card. Discuss its use with the class.
2. Find out when your local children's clinic is held. Ask the nurse if you may visit it and watch what happens.
3. Write a story, with pictures, about your day at the clinic.

4 Draw a poster telling mothers about the children's clinic. Do not forget to say the time, the day and where it is held.
5 Draw a poster about *one* of the six diseases: measles; diptheria; tetanus; polio; TB or whooping cough.

Polio immunisation prevents this

What should children eat?

Babies and children need good food to help them grow, learn, play and to protect them from diseases. If a baby is not fed well then she will not grow. She will become weak and sick and be less clever. Children need lots of food to make them strong and bright.

What is the best food?

From birth to two years the best food is breast-milk. But at 4 months a baby needs more than just breast-milk on its own. She also needs other food. If the baby is very big or a twin then she may need food before she is 4 months.

A child needs a mixture of foods

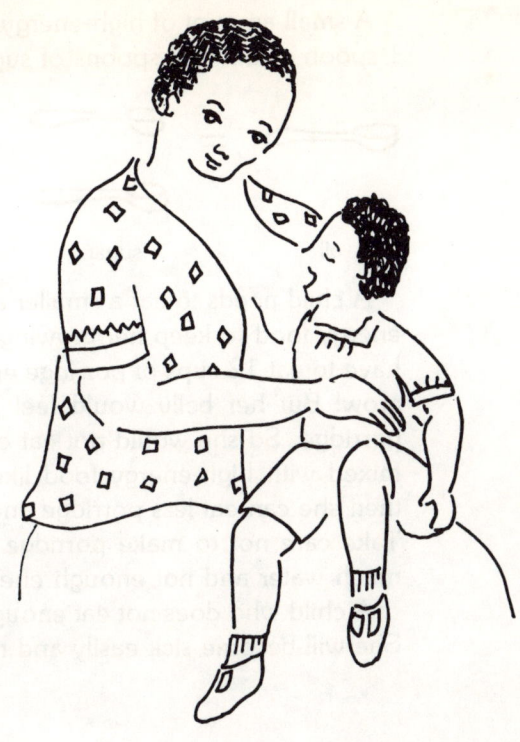

Breast-feed until the child is two years old

Energy food Different foods help us in different ways. Babies and children need food that gives them **energy**. Energy food helps children grow, play and keep alert. Some foods are **high-energy** and some foods are **low-energy**.

High-energy	cooking oil	flying ants
	palm oil	beans
	margarine	sunflower seeds or oil
	ground-nut butter	pumpkin seeds
	ground-nut oil	sesame seeds
	lard, cooking fat	nuts
	bread	rapoko
Low-energy	maize meal	cassava
	porridge (of millet, sorghum or maize)	sugar cane
		yams
	bananas	plantains
	potatoes	avocado pears
	rice	dried peas and beans

29

A small amount of high-energy food equals a lot of low-energy food. 1 spoon of oil = 2 spoons of sugar = 5 spoons of maize porridge.

oil
sugar
maize porridge

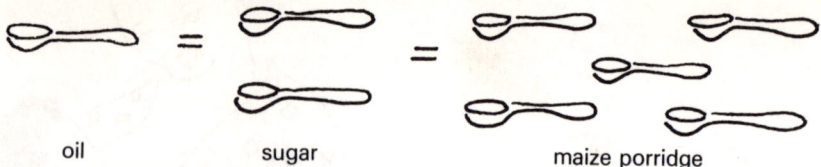

A child needs to eat a smaller amount of high-energy food than low-energy food to keep her growing and healthy. A 2 year-old girl would have to eat 12 cups of porridge every day to give her enough energy to grow! But her belly would feel full before she had eaten that much porridge. So she would not eat enough energy food. If the porridge is mixed with high-energy food like ground-nut butter or sunflower oil, then she can eat less porridge and still have enough energy every day. Take care not to make porridge too thin because you have used too much water and not enough energy-giving cereal.

A child who does not eat enough food will sit and do nothing all day. She will become sick easily and not grow well.

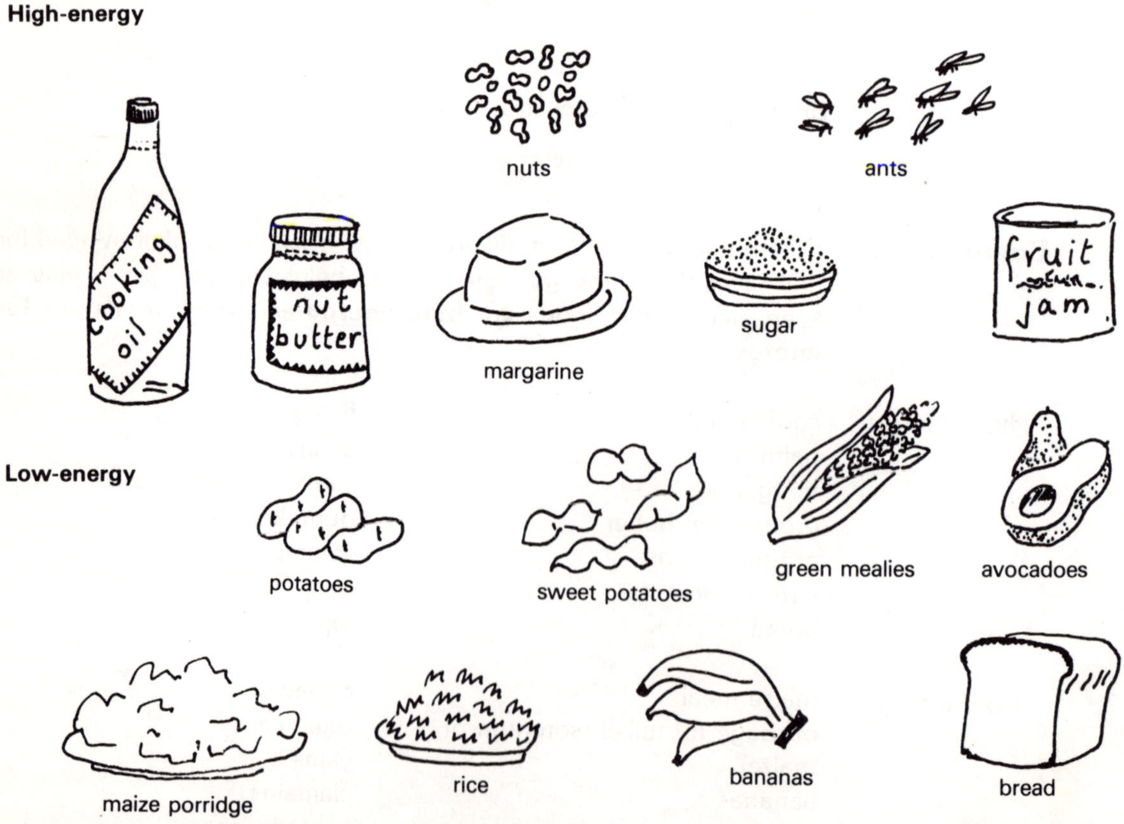

High-energy
nuts
ants
cooking oil
nut butter
margarine
sugar
fruit jam
Low-energy
potatoes
sweet potatoes
green mealies
avocadoes
maize porridge
rice
bananas
bread

Energy foods

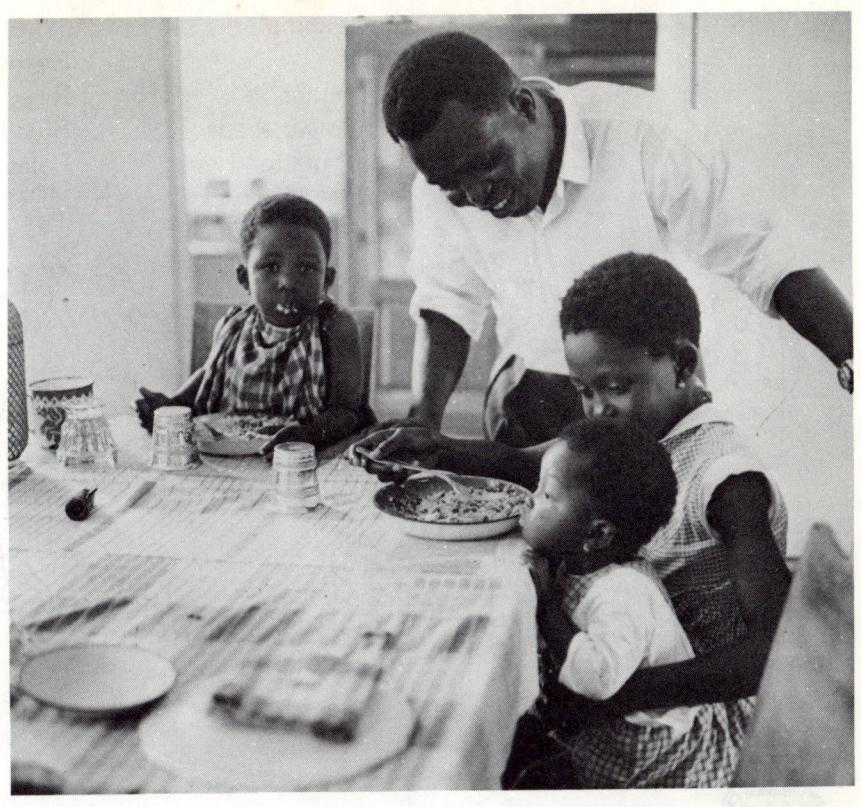

Growing food

Children also need **growing food**. This type of food helps all parts of the child to grow into a strong healthy adult. Skin, bones, hair, brains, teeth and muscles all need growing food. Adults need growing food so that their hair and skin keeps growing and wounds heal well.

Growing foods

eggs
kidney beans
soya beans
yogurt
sour milk
peas
meat
cheese
rice
whole wheat bread

snails
nuts
milk
insects (caterpillars, ants, locusts)
fish
millet, sorghum, sesame
ground-nuts
shellfish

We all need some growing food, with our energy food every day. Energy foods help growing foods do their work. Growing foods work better when they are mixed.

Here are some examples:
Nuts and insects
Bread and nut butter
Beans and sunflower seeds
Beans, nuts and maize
Beans and rice
Rice, sesame seeds and insects
Bread and cheese
Potatoes, millet and milk
Millet and milk

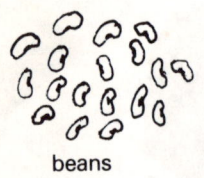
beans

flying ants

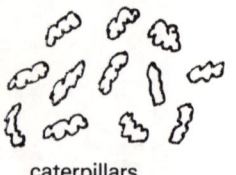
caterpillars

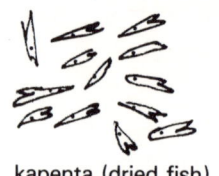
kapenta (dried fish)

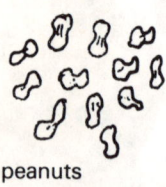
peanuts

meat

chicken

fish

nut butter

dried green leaves

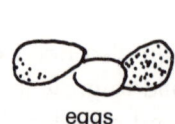
eggs

milk curds   milk

Growing foods

Protective foods

Protective foods are needed every day to protect us from diseases and to keep our eyes, skin and hair shining and healthy. A child who eats no 'shining' food would have poor eyesight and be sick often. Some protective food should be eaten every day.

Protective foods

Vegetables: pumpkins, cabbage, rape, kale, pumpkin leaves, peanuts, potatoes, fresh maize, carrots, onions, tomatoes, sprouting beans, fresh herbs, green beans, peas, watercress, peppers, sweet potato leaves, spinach.
Fruit: mangoes, oranges, lemons, guava, avocado pears, paw-paw, peaches, apricots, apples, wild fruit, mulberries, blackcurrants, pineapple.
Others: nuts, ground-nuts and other pulses, milk, eggs, margarine, liver, meat, fish and wholemeal cereals

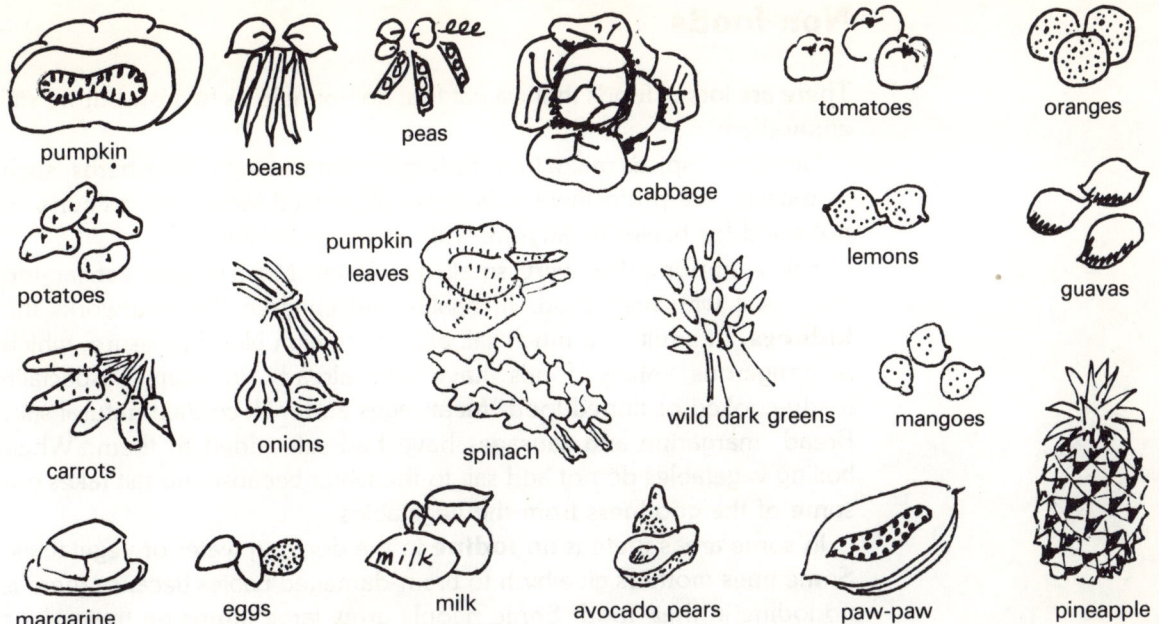

'Shining' foods

Some foods are good for growth and give energy. Other foods help with protecting and growing. Pulses, such as ground-nuts and whole meal cereals, are energy, growing *and* protective foods. They are good, inexpensive foods but we could not live on nothing but ground-nuts or cereals. We all need a *mixture* of good foods. This is called a **balanced diet**.

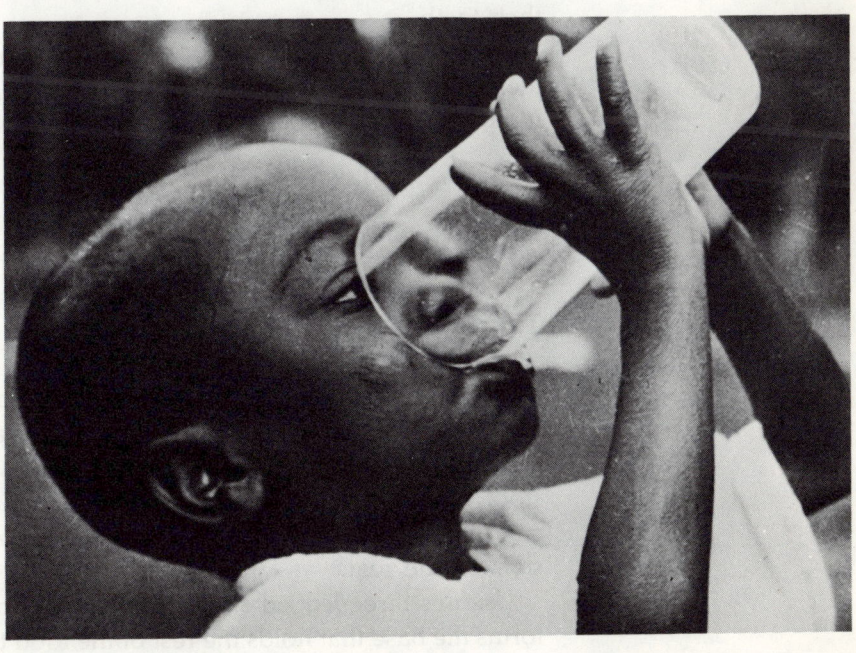

Non-foods

There are lots of foods that we eat that do not help us to grow but we still enjoy them.

Herbs and spices make food taste more interesting. Fresh herbs, such as parsley, are protective foods. Strongly-spiced food, such as curry, is not good for babies or anyone with an upset stomach.

Salt is important in very small quantities. Most people eat far too much salt with their food. In babies and children this overworks the **kidneys**. In adults too much salt can cause high blood pressure, which is dangerous. Many foods have salt already in them, especially ready-cooked or tinned food. Meat, eggs and milk contain natural salt. Bread, margarine and sausages have had salt added to them. When boiling vegetables do not add salt to the water because the salt takes out some of the goodness from the vegetables.

In some areas there is no **iodine** in the drinking water or vegetables. Sometimes mothers give birth to brain-damaged babies because there is no iodine in their food. Some people grow large lumps on their necks because they have eaten no iodine. Salt can be bought with iodine added to it. If people eat too much salt then they forget what food really tastes of. Try eating food with no salt on it and enjoy the fresh taste.

Tea and coffee do no harm and cheer one up at the end of the day. Sometimes tea or coffee stop children from falling asleep at night. Strong tea or coffee is not good for children, especially at bed time.

Sweet, fizzy drinks ('cool-drinks') are an expensive way of drinking coloured, sweetened water with bubbles of air. If children drink fizzy drinks often, then holes, which will be ugly and painful, will appear in their teeth.

Sweets are high in energy, but they are also expensive and rot the teeth. When anyone wants a snack peanuts, a boiled egg or bread and margarine are better to eat than sweets.

The three-legged stool for healthy eating

This is an idea to help in learning how to make good meals.

The seat of the stool is the main food (maize with breast-milk) The three legs are energy foods, growing foods and protective foods. The round seat can be made from cardboard or wood. Make the legs of the stool with cardboard rectangles. Draw on them all the foods that you can find in you area. Cut the tops of the cards to make tabs to fit the slots on the seat.

Use this three-legged stool to make balanced meals. The main food forms the base that holds the rest of the food together. Without the legs,

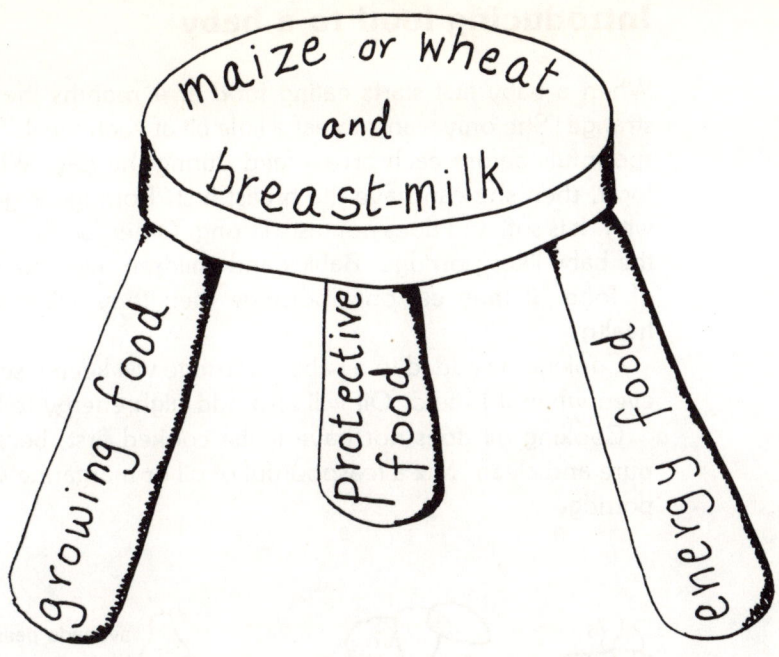

The three-legged stool for healthy eating: the main food forms the base and all three helper foods are needed to hold the stool up

the stool would fall over. If this happened to a child's meals the child would fall sick.

Here is another way of showing that a mixture of foods is needed: The cooking pot is the main food, for example maize porridge or rice. The three rocks that hold it up are energy food, growing food and protective food. If one rock is taken away, then the cooking pot will fall over. If one type of food is taken away, then the child will fall sick.

Introducing food to a baby

When a baby first starts eating food at 4 months the taste and feel is strange. She only wants to eat a little bit at each meal. She can eat a few spoonfuls before each breast-feed during the day. When she likes the food, then she can have the breast first. Porridge is good food to start with. It is soft and does not taste strong. Other foods can be added when the baby likes porridge. Babies and children need many different types of food. If they eat only porridge then they will not grow and stay healthy.

Cooking oil added to a baby's porridge will keep it soft enough to eat, even when it is cold. Oil will also add high energy to the porridge.

Cooking oil does not have to be cooked first, because it is already pure and clean. Mix a teaspoonful of oil or margarine with each bowl of porridge.

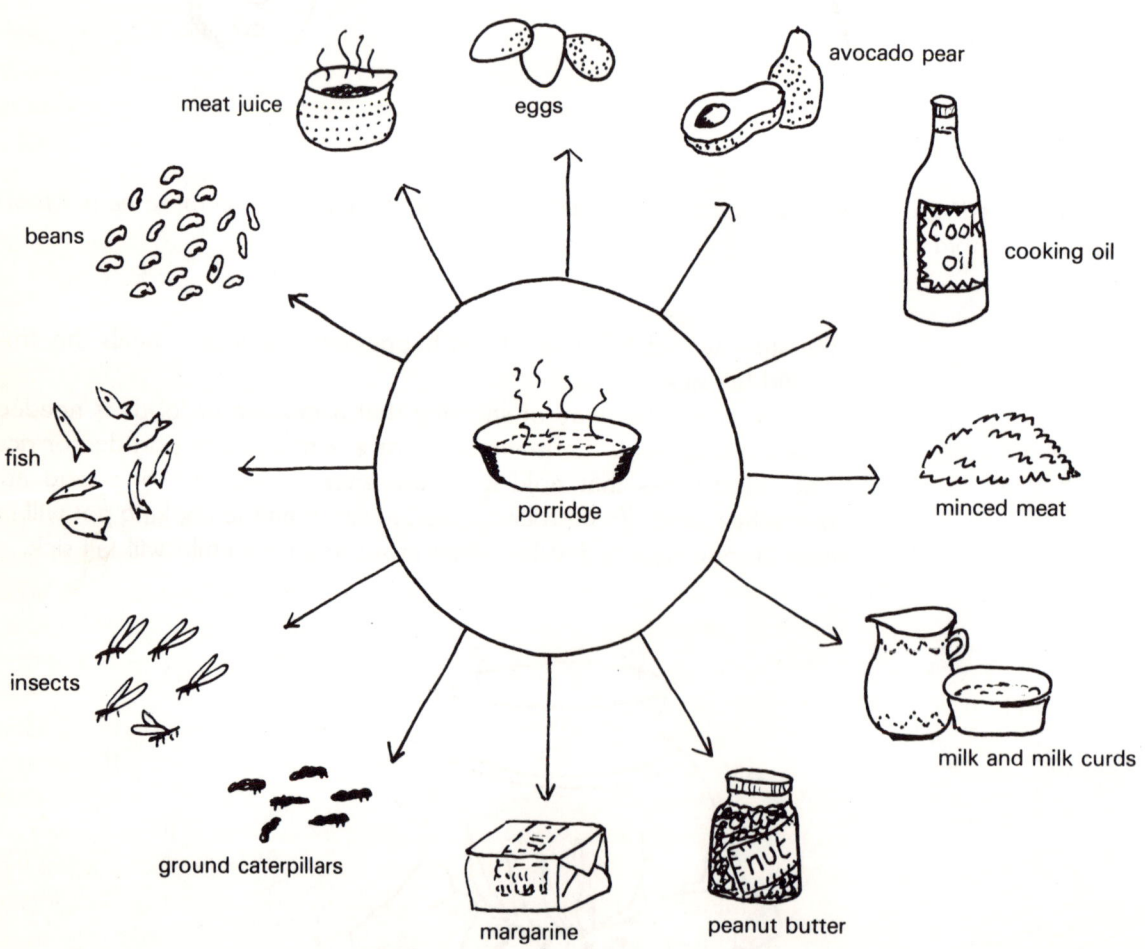

With porridge, give a baby . . .

Home-made baby foods

Some parents do not have enough money to buy cooking oil or there is no shop near their home; but everyone can grow ground-nuts, pumpkin seeds or sunflower seeds. These are all full of both high-energy and growing foods and ground-nut butter is delicious and easy for a baby to eat. It is cheap for mothers to make or buy.

Special baby food from shops is easy to use, but it is expensive. Mothers can make baby food cheaply and easily. They need not spend their money on baby food in packets or tins. Food that all the family eats can be mashed so it is soft enough for the baby. A child with only a few teeth does not chew food well. The seeds from a fresh maize cob, or sunflower seeds will pass straight through the stomach. They must be pounded first.

The green leaves of pumpkin, sweet potato, peas or cabbage can be dried in the sun. When they are dry and crisp they are pounded into a powder and kept in a closed tin or jar. A big spoonful of this powder can be added to the porridge while it is being cooked. Mashed avocado pear, paw-paw, pumpkin, bananas and potatoes are good for small children and babies. A spoonful of dried milk added to the porridge is good but dried milk should never be given to a baby in a bottle. Pounded dried fish and minced meat are also good growing foods for babies.

Babies and small children have small stomachs so they need lots of small meals every day.

> CHILDREN ARE LIKE CHICKENS: THEY SHOULD ALWAYS BE PECKING.
> MORE FOOD = MORE CHILD

Not only the child's body is growing fast. For the first two years the brain is growing too. If a child does not eat enough food during her first two years then her brain will not grow properly. She will always be slow and dull. A half-grown brain cannot grow later, even if good food is given later. So it is especially important that a baby is fed well in the first two years.

School-children need food during the day to help them work. Snack foods such as sweets, biscuits, potato chips and sweet fizzy drinks are not good for growing children. They are also expensive. Sweets and sweet fizzy drinks make teeth rot. A boiled fresh maize cob and a bag of ground-nuts, or a boiled egg and some bananas make a good meal for school-children. Hungry children are tired children. Tired children cannot think so well about their school-work.

Taking food to school

Malnutrition

A child of two years is half the height of an adult. Her brain has finished growing. This is why good food is so important for young children. If a child is not fed enough then she will not grow and she will be sick often. Poor feeding kills more children than any disease. Children need 3 meals a day, or more if they are malnourished. Children who do not eat enough become malnourished. Their hair grows thin and pale. Their arms and legs are very thin. Sometimes their hands and feet become swollen with water and their skin peels. This is called **kwashiorkor**. These children will need special care and food to grow strong again. Catching up later is always more difficult. Many people are small and slow all their lives because they did not get enough to eat when they were children.

The measuring strip

Here is an easy way to find out if children are well fed:
The thickness of a child's upper arm does not change much between the ages of one and five years. But a well-fed child has a thicker upper arm than a malnourished child. By measuring around the child's arm, we can find out if the child is well fed, too thin or dangerously malnourished.

Measure and make lines on a strip of thick paper, plastic or thin card. Mark the strip with ball-point pen or coloured pencils.

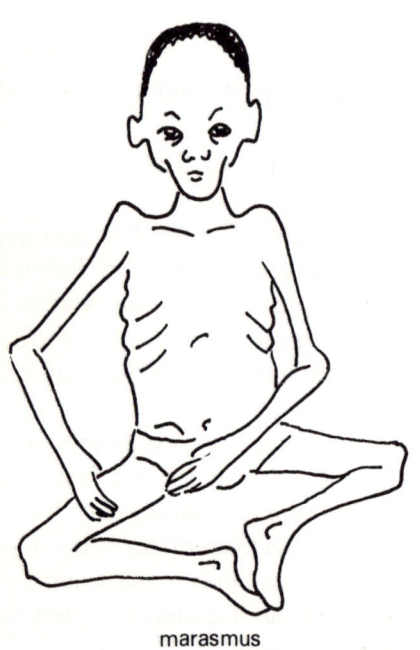
marasmus

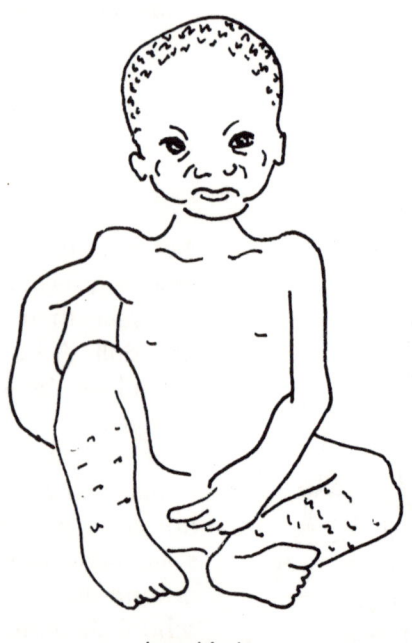
kwashiorkor

Undernourished children

Measure the upper arms of children between one and five years old.
If the upper arm is over 14 cm then the child is well fed.
If the upper arm is less than 14 cm then the child is thin.
If the upper arm is less than 12½ cm then the child is malnourished.

Practise measuring on pieces of round wood or on rolls of cardboard or paper. Use pieces that vary in thickness from 11 cm to 15 cm round. Write a child's name on each piece. Then pretend that the pieces of wood or cardboard are different children's arms. Which 'children' are healthy and which are too thin?

You can also learn to measure the upper arm of children with your fingers. With a piece of wood that you know to be 14 cm find out how far round your fingers reach. Then try it with other pieces of wood and see how they feel.

See who can tell which children are healthy and which are too thin. Put different sized rolls of wood or paper in a bag. Try and discover which ones are too thin by feeling the rolls inside the bag without looking.

Measuring upper arm thickness

Children who are too thin, or malnourished, need more food. Sometimes their parents cannot feed them well because they are too poor. Perhaps the father has no job, the family does not have enough land or there have been no rains this year. One thing that a family can do to make their children grow is to give them *more* food every day. A child with an upper arm measurement of less than 14 cm needs at least 4 or 5 meals every day.

Sometimes parents have grown lots of food but they sell the crops for money. With the money they get for gound-nuts or sunflowers they buy bread and biscuits. The family would be healthier and stronger if they ate more of their crops and only sold what they really do not need for the rest of the year.

Sometimes the parents have enough money to buy food, but they have not learnt about balanced meals. They spend the money on new shoes or beer and the children eat only maize or cassava. When the son falls sick from kwashiorkor he is taken to an expensive private doctor for treatment. The doctor may give him injections, which the child does not need. The treatment he needs is in the shops and fields: balanced meals of good food!

Making peanut butter

40

Gardens

Schools can help teach the whole community about good feeding by keeping a vegetable and fruit garden. Even the youngest school-children can help in the garden. They can water it using tins, plastic bottles or gourds. They can learn which plants are weeds and help to pull them up. They can remove locusts and caterpillars, which can be fed to the chickens.

Parents can see and taste new vegetables before they try them in their own gardens. They can learn about moving the vegetables around the garden each year.

A school garden needs to be near someone's house to prevent theft. Cattle and goats have to be kept out with a strong fence. In the holidays students will have to take turns in watering the garden.

Rabbits and guinea-pigs for meat, and chickens for eggs can be kept at school. In this way students and parents can all learn how to look after them. The manure from the animals is good fertiliser for the vegetable garden. The chickens and rabbits will need strong pens to prevent theft or attack from wild animals. Rabbits and guinea-pigs are easy to keep, even in an urban school. They can be fed with vegetables which have been thrown away by markets and shops.

If there is no land to grow vegetables on, then many types of vegetables can be grown is pots, barrels, clay pipes, boxes, drums or plastic sacks. A car tyre turned inside out can be used to make a small garden.

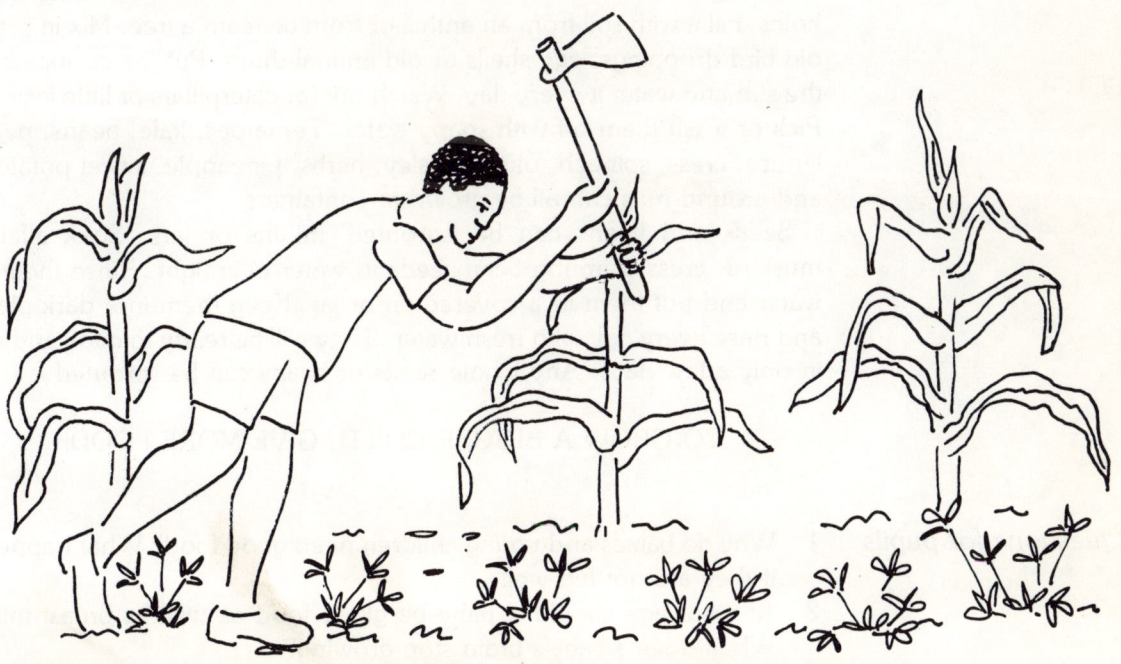

Put big stones at the bottom of the container and make some drainage holes. Fill it with soil from an anthill or from beneath a tree. Mix in some old bird droppings, egg shells or old animal dung. Put the container in the sun and water it every day. Watch out for caterpillars or little insects. Pick or wash them off with soapy water. Tomatoes, kale, beans, peas, lettuce, cress, spinach, okra, parsley, herbs, pineapple, sweet potatoes and ground-nuts can all be grown in containers.

Seeds and beans can be 'sprouted' in tins or jars. Soak alfalfa, mustard, cress or mung bean seeds in water overnight. Rinse them in water and put them in a covered tin or jar. Keep them in a dark place and rinse every day with fresh water. They will be ready to cook and eat in only a few days. Any whole seeds or beans can be sprouted.

TO GROW A BIGGER CHILD, GIVE MORE FOOD!

Questions for pupils

1 Why do babies and young children need good food? What happens if they are not fed well?
2 At what age should a baby be given food as well as breast-milk? When does a baby's brain stop growing?

3 How many meals should a child between 2 and 5 years old eat every day?
4 Draw some food that is good for children. Name each food.
5 Draw a picture of food that is not good for children.

Activities for pupils

1 Find two caterpillars. Put one in a jar with lots of leaves. Put the other in a jar with only some water. Which caterpillar grows best? Write a story about the two caterpillars.
2 Visit your local shop or market. Write two lists of food: the good foods that help us grow and keep healthy and the bad foods that waste our money.
Find out the prices of the food. How many eggs can you buy for the same price as a soft fizzy drink? How much milk can you buy for the same price as a packet of potato chips?

Examples:

Good	**Bad**
Bananas, oil, eggs, milk cabbage, maize meal, carrots, paw-paw	Coke, sweet biscuits, bubblegum, sweets, beer, cream soda drink

Find out the prices of the food. How many eggs can you buy for the same price as a soft fizzy drink? How much milk can you buy for the same price as a packet of potato chips?
3 Make some healthy snacks for school children.
4 Grow some ground-nuts and share them with your friends. Tell them why ground-nuts are better then bubble-gum.
5 Ask your teacher if the school can start a vegetable garden.
6 Make a three-legged stool to show balanced meals.
7 Make some porridge for a baby. Add some cooking oil. What happens? Why is cooking oil good for growing babies?

Why do we keep clean?

Germs

Keeping clean is the simplest way of preventing many diseases. Sickness and disease are caused by **germs**. These are so small that we cannot see them with our eyes, but they are everywhere. Germs are alive. They like dirty places. Hospitals have very few germs in them because nurses frequently clean everything. Homes that are never cleaned have many germs in them. Germs cannot grow in clean places.

People breathe germs in from the air, by touching other people or by touching things that have germs on them, such as dirty towels. People swallow germs in dirty water or rotten food. If a person is strong and fed well then he can fight off many of the diseases that germs carry. A weak or malnourished child will not be able to fight diseases. He may become sick or even die.

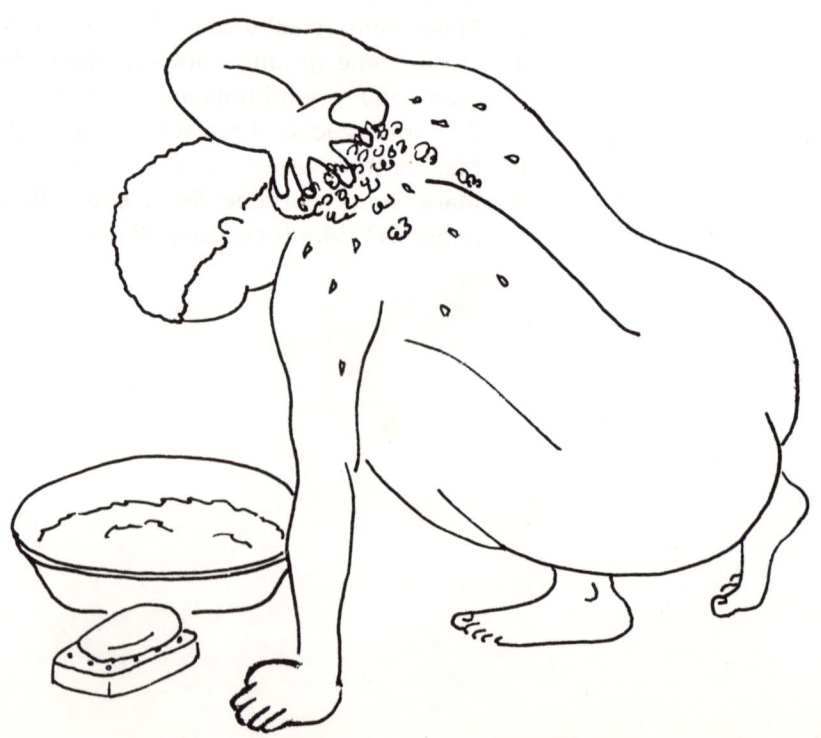

Always wash hands before eating and after using the toilet

Using a latrine prevents this!

There are many thousands of germs in faeces. If someone does not wash their hands often they will carry these germs on their hands. They may pass the germs onto someone else.

A child who has diarrhoea may not wash his hands after going to the toilet. He gives a piece of bread to a friend. His fingers are covered with diarrhoea germs, which are so small that they cannot be seen. Some of the germs stick to the bread. When his friend eats the bread, he is eating diarrhoea germs too. The next day the friend has diarrhoea. Is it kind to give someone else a present of germs?

Animals and people

Animals, such as dogs and chickens, can spread germs. If children do not use a **latrine**, but defecate on the ground, a dog may walk in the faeces. The dog then enters the home, carrying the germs on its feet. In the home a baby is crawling on the floor. The germs go onto his hands and knees. The mother picks up the baby to feed it and then she starts to cook the family meal, without washing her hands first. The family eats the meal — and the germs. Soon the whole family might have diarrhoea or worms.

What can be done?

Everyone should use a toilet or latrine. If a small child defecates on the ground, then the faeces should be cleared-up quickly, before anyone walks in them. Keep a special toilet pot in the house for small children. Empty it into the latrine whenever it is used.

Flies

Faeces left on the ground get covered with flies. Flies breed in warm, wet places like piles of rubbish and uncovered latrines. Flies carry germs on their feet. First they walk in faeces and then they walk on our food. The germs stick to the food, where they grow and multiply. You cannot see or taste germs. But they make you sick later. Get rid of flies by keeping the inside and outside of homes clean. Cover all food and water. Uncovered food and dirty places attract flies. Keep all food in a box or covered with a cloth.

Never eat food that is old or smells bad: it may be poisonous and full of germs. Meat should always be well-cooked, especially pig meat. Raw pig meat can carry dangerous diseases or worm eggs.

Fresh fruit and vegetables should be washed before eating. Do not allow children to eat food that has been dropped on the floor: it may be covered in germs.

Rubbish

Do not keep old food and rubbish in the home. Burn the rubbish and give the food scraps to the chickens. Each village or groups of homes

should have a rubbish pit. The rubbish should be burned in the pit every day. Anything that does not burn can be covered with soil. Dig the pit away from the home.

Clean water

Drinking-water from streams or ponds should always be boiled. This will kill the germs. After boiling the water keep it in a covered pot to prevent germs and flies from falling in. Another way to kill the germs is to put the water in a glass, see-through plastic bottle or bag and leave it in the sun for at least two hours.

Personal Cleanliness

Spitting on the floor spreads germs and diseases. Spit has many thousands of germs in it, especially if the person is sick. People should cover their mouths with their hands when they cough or sneeze. Wash handkerchiefs every day and hang them in the sun to dry.

Germs and worm eggs can hide in long finger nails. Keep them cut short. Bath or wash all over the body every day. Bathing with soap prevents skin infections, rashes and itching. Bathing also makes people smell nicer! If a child is old enough to bath himself, check that he really has washed. Children often say they have washed when they have not!

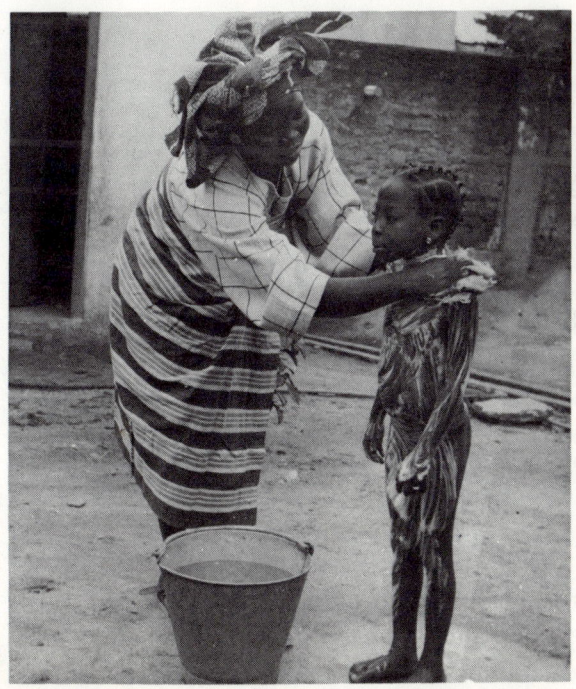

Teeth

Teeth are a very important part of our bodies. We need them for biting and chewing our food. We need them for smiling and talking clearly. A child with shining white teeth looks happy and attractive.

At about 7 years of age the first set of teeth fall out. New, bigger teeth grow in their place. These are the last teeth we have. We must look after them well.

Brush teeth every day after meals and after eating sweet foods. Sweets and food stuck between the teeth make them rot. Rotten teeth are painful and ugly. Once a tooth gets a small hole in it the hole will grow bigger. The hole fills up with food, which makes the tooth rot more. The hole has to be filled with metal by a **dentist** to prevent it growing bigger. Very rotten teeth have to be pulled out. They will not grow again.

Toothbrush — You can make a toothbrush with a stick from a tree. Gum (eucalyptus) sticks taste the best. Chew one end of the stick until it is soft and hairy. Use it to brush the teeth and gums. Brush all over the teeth and gums, especially at the back and in the corners. If you have a knife, sharpen one end of the stick to a point and use this to clean between the teeth. Instead of toothpaste you can use an equal mixture of salt and bicarbonate of soda (baking powder). Dip the wet toothbrush into this and brush all over.

To show that sugar and sweet food makes teeth rot

You will need two teeth for this. Ask a child who is losing his first teeth for his. Put one tooth in a bottle of fizzy sweet drink, like Cola. Put the other tooth in a bottle of water. Leave them for two weeks. The tooth in the Cola drink will be going soft. You can scrape bits off with a knife. The tooth in the water is still strong and healthy.

All foods with sugar in them make teeth rot: sweets, sweet drinks, bubble gum, biscuits, even sugar-cane. Eat some ground-nuts or a banana or drink a cup of milk instead.

Public cleanliness

As well as our bodies and food we must also keep our houses, streets and villages clean. Public cleanliness is called **sanitation.**

Drinking water

The most common way for germs to spread from one person to another, or from animals to people, is through drinking water. Drinking water from a tap is not possible for everybody, but wells and springs can be kept clean. Wells need a fence around them to prevent animals from falling into the water. People might not notice that there was a dead animal in the well. Then it would rot and everyone would become sick from drinking the water.

Animals can put germs into springs and water-holes with their feet and tongues if they drink from them. Springs and water-holes need a fence around them too. Best of all, drinking water sources should be covered and the water taken out with a pump. People must not go to the toilet near a source of drinking water. The germs can easily be washed into the water by the rain.

Water can also become poisonous in towns and cities. Factories may pour dangerous chemicals into the river and people a few kilometres downstream drink the river water. The **sewage** from a city may be poured into a river or the sea. Bathing or drinking nearby would be very dangerous.

Some rivers have so many chemicals poured into them that all the fish and river plants die. Sometimes so much chemical **fertiliser** from the fields is washed into the rivers that the plants grow too fast. Then the river becomes so full of plants that the fish die and boats cannot travel on the river.

Latrines Build latrines and make sure everyone uses them. Each family should have its own latrine. They must be at least 20 m away from all homes, wells, springs, rivers and streams. Latrines can be built of many different materials. In some areas wooden poles for the walls with grass-thatched roofs are the cheapest materials. In other areas trees are scarce, so clay bricks are used for the walls.

A 'Blair' pit latrine has a pipe going from a hole in the floor up to above the roof. This pipe takes smells from the pit underneath and catches flies in a net at the top. If the latrine is dark inside then flies will not go into it. Small children are sometimes frightened of going into dark places. They think they will fall into the hole. Someone can go with them until they know that it is safe.

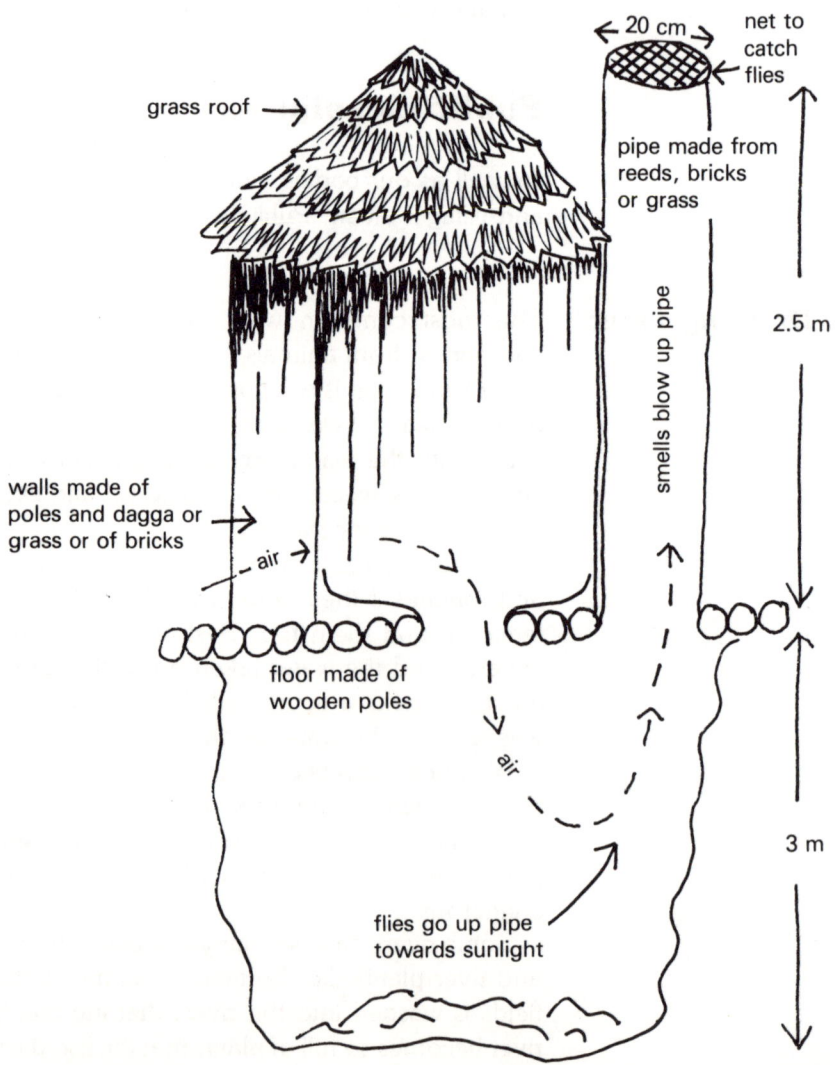

A Blair Pit Latrine

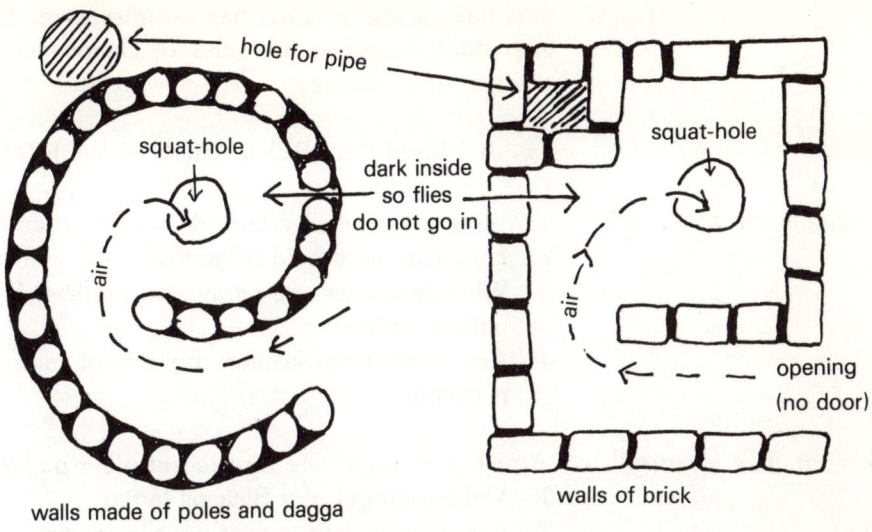

Plans of a Blair Pit Latrines

Clean air As well as good food and clean water we all need clean air to breathe. We only spend a part of each day eating and drinking but we are breathing all day and night. If we do some hard work or run around we breathe faster and deeper. We need fresh, clean air to keep alive and healthy.

Cars, lorries and factories produce poisonous, dirty air. People who live in cities or near busy roads breathe in this dirty air and may get dangerous diseases. There are many jobs that are dangerous because of the air people have to breathe. People who dig up or make things out of **asbestos** often get a disease that disables and then kills them because they breathe in very small amounts of the asbestos.

Smoke from a cooking fire is not good for the lungs. If there is no chimney then the door or windows should be kept open. Never go to sleep in a room with a fire and the windows closed. You might never wake up again. Keep babies and anyone with a cough out of smokey rooms and away from paraffin stoves.

Rubbish Public cleanliness also means not leaving rubbish lying around in the streets, fields and villages. Rubbish attracts flies which breed there and make more flies. Plastic bags left lying around could be eaten by animals. This will kill them. Plastic never rots as old vegetables do. Plastic just stays where it is left – for ever. Broken bottles and rusty tins can cut people's feet. They also collect water where mosquitoes can breed.

A tidy village or street has less disease and looks more attractive. If everybody keeps to the rules of cleanliness there will be much less sickness and disease.

A GRAM OF PREVENTION IS WORTH A KILO OF CURE

Questions for pupils
1. What are germs? Where do we find them?
2. How can we get rid of germs?
3. Why should we use latrines and toilets? Where is the best place to build a latrine?
4. Are there flies around the school latrine? How could they be prevented?

Activities for pupils

Activities marked* are directed at older pupils and teachers
1. Make a model of a Blair pit latrine.*
2. If there is no latrine near your home try to get some people to help you build one.*
3. Make up a play with your class about the need to keep clean. Act it in your village or street.
4. Make some toothbrushes with green sticks. Show younger children how to use them.*
5. If water has to be fetched a long way from your home, would it be possible to build a well nearby? Ask your local council for help.*
6. Show young children how to wash their hands and faces before eating and after using the toilet. Clean their teeth after eating.*
7. Have a rubbish collecting day. See how tidy you can make your community.
8. Dig a rubbish pit near your home or school. Use it every day.*

7 Sickness and health

A healthy baby or child gives everyone pleasure to watch. She is active, playful, sucks at the breast and eats well. She is interested in what goes on around her. The healthy baby has strong arms and legs, bright eyes, firm smooth skin and black shining hair. She smiles often and sleeps well. If you know a healthy baby then you will quickly notice any changes that show she is sick. Here are some signs of sickness:

LOOK with your EYES
Loss of interest — the child does not want to play
Not eating or sucking well
Rashes, lumps, swelling on the skin
Red or sore eyes
Sores and cuts
Shaking or sudden strange movements
Rapid breathing
Unusual sleepiness
Stiffness in the neck or limbs
Pain when one part of the body is moved.
Holding one or both ears

FEEL with your HANDS
Fever, or hot body
Very thin arms
Skin that stays wrinkled after pinching
Hot ears or other part of the body

LISTEN with your EARS
A different cry
Difficult breathing
Coughing and wheezing

SMELL with your NOSE
Smelly sores
Smelly ears
Watery faeces that smell bad

The MOST DANGEROUS signs of sickness are:
Very fast or noisy breathing
Fever which lasts more than three days
Blood in the faeces, urine or spit
Very high fever and wandering mind
Diarrhoea for several days and no urine

All these signs are more dangerous if the child is very thin or malnourished.

Caring for the sick child

All children are sick sometimes. If we know what to do then we can prevent them from becoming very sick or dying. A strong, well-fed child will not get ill as often as a weak, malnourished child. The weak child will take longer to get better.

Sick children need feeding even more than well children. When a child is sick he needs extra food to help fight the disease. High fever is like a hot fire. It uses up a lot of energy foods like a hot fire uses fuel. In a 3 hour attack of malaria a person burns up as much energy as a farm worker needs for 8 hours of work! The sick child needs to eat enough energy food to put back what is burned up by the fever. If the child is not fed enough, then the fever will burn up the sick child's body. He will become thinner and grow very weak.

Feed ill children often

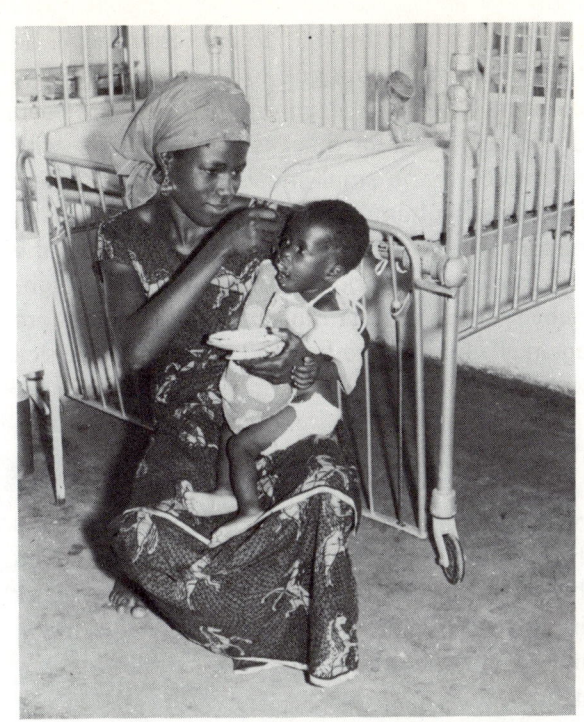 

GIVE SICK CHILDREN PLENTY TO EAT AND DRINK

Many diseases stop a child from wanting to eat. Some diseases, like measles, make a child's mouth sore so that eating is painful. Sometimes the child feels too weak to eat. A sick child can quickly become malnourished. If he is sick for some weeks or has several short attacks of sickness, he is in special danger.

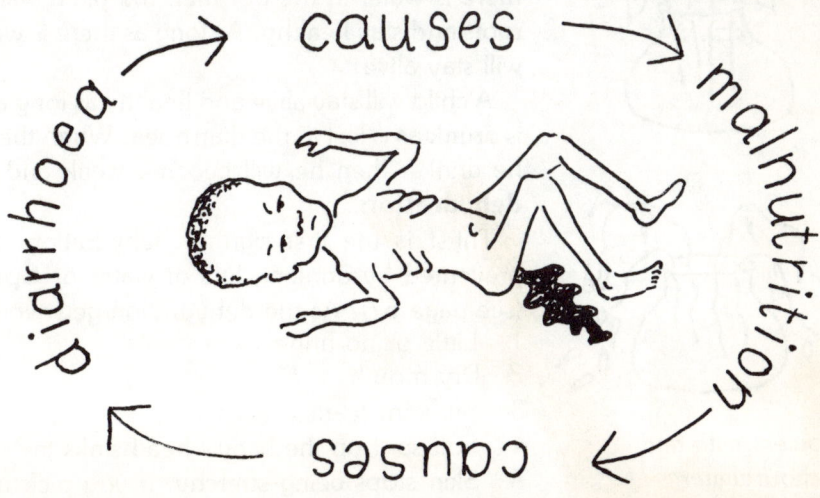

The mother of a sick child must help the child to eat, especially if he has a fever or diarrhoea. Babies must continue to be breast-fed. The child can eat any foods that he likes. Soft, high-energy foods are best: peanut butter; avocado pear; scrambled eggs or porridge with margarine. The sick child needs many small meals rather than a few large ones: he needs little meals often. When the child's sickness is gone, he is only partly better. He is not completely better until he is the same weight as he was before he was sick. He needs plenty of high-energy foods. If he is a baby then his mother must breast-feed him more often until he is strong again. If children are fed well when they are sick they will get better more quickly.

BREAST-FEED ALL SICK BABIES

Diarrhoea This is the most common sickness among children. Babies who are fed with bottles have diarrhoea more often then breast-fed babies. Even strong healthy children have diarrhoea sometimes but they will get better quickly. Weak or malnourished children may die from diarrhoea. Diarrhoea kills more children in Africa than any other sickness.

The main causes of diarrhoea are:
1 Poor feeding
2 Not washing hands before eating
3 Rotten food
4 Dirty drinking water
5 Dirty kitchen tools
6 Flies carrying germs onto food
7 Worms in the belly

This sickness of diarrhoea does not kill children. What is harmful is losing so much water from the body. This must be put back into the body as fast as it is lost.

If a plant in a pot is given no water then it will soon wilt and die. If there is water in the pot then the plant will drink the water through its roots and stay healthy. As long as there is water in the pot then the plant will stay alive.

A child will stay alive and healthy as long as the same amount of water is drunk as is lost in the diarrhoea. When the child loses more water then he drinks, then he will become weak and perhaps die. This is called **dehydration**.

Thirst is the first sign of dehydration. Dehydration can easily be prevented by drinking lots of water or **Special Rehydration Drink** (see page 57). As the dehydration gets worse there will be other signs:
1 Little or no urine
2 Dry mouth
3 Sunken, tearless eyes
4 Soft spot on the baby's head sinks in
5 Skin stops being stretchy. If you pick up some of the skin on the

Flowers with and without water

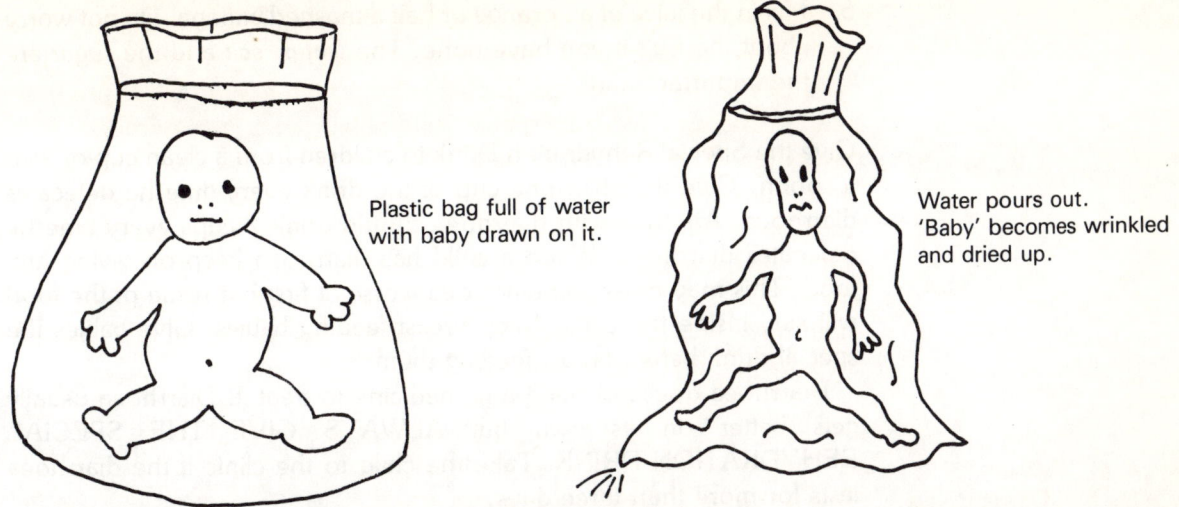

Plastic bag full of water with baby drawn on it.

Water pours out. 'Baby' becomes wrinkled and dried up.

How to show drying-up from diarrhoea

back of your hand it will quickly spring back; in a dehydrated child the skin stays pinched up.

A dehydrated child needs to drink the Special Rehydration Drink fast. *Anyone* with diarrhoea or vomiting must drink the Special Rehydration Drink. This drink can be used to *prevent* and to *treat* dehydration.

Special Rehydration Drink

1 Find a family-sized soft fizzy drink bottle (720 ml) and wash it out.
2 Fill the bottle with *clean* drinking water.
3 Mix in ½ teaspoon of salt.
4 *Taste* the drink. It should taste like tears. If it is more salty than tears, then throw it away and start again.
5 Mix in 6 teaspoons of sugar.

TASTE special drink

Ingredients for Special Rehydration Drink

6 Mix in the juice of an orange or half a mashed banana. Do not worry about the fruit if you have none. The *water*, *salt* and the *sugar* are the important parts.

Give the Special Rehydration Drink to children from a clean cup or with a spoon. Give the child one cup of the drink every time he defecates diarrhoea. An adult with diarrhoea should drink 2 cups every time he defecates diarrhoea. When a child has diarrhoea keep on giving him food. This may make the diarrhoea worse at first but some of the food will stay inside the child. Keep breast-feeding babies. Give babies the special drink before breast-feeding them.

Diarrhoea does not need any medicine to treat it. Diarrhoea usually gets better on its own but ALWAYS GIVE THE SPECIAL REHYDRATION DRINK. Take the child to the clinic if the diarrhoea lasts for more than three days.

Vomiting Many people **vomit** when they have an upset stomach. Usually it is not serious and gets better on its own. The danger is dehydration. The child should not eat anything while he is vomiting but he must drink. Give him the Special Rehydration Drink in small sips. Do not let him gulp down all of it at once. He will not vomit it all back. Some of the drink will stay inside him. If vomiting continues for more than a day, take the child to a clinic.

Fevers Fevers can be caused by many diseases. Sometimes a baby has a fever because she is wearing too many clothes on a hot day! A child with a fever needs to be cooled down. If the fever goes too high then the child could die or have **fits**. Do not wrap up a child with blankets when he has a fever. Take his clothes off. If he is very hot fan him with a newspaper and wipe him all over with a wet cloth. Do this until he is cooler.

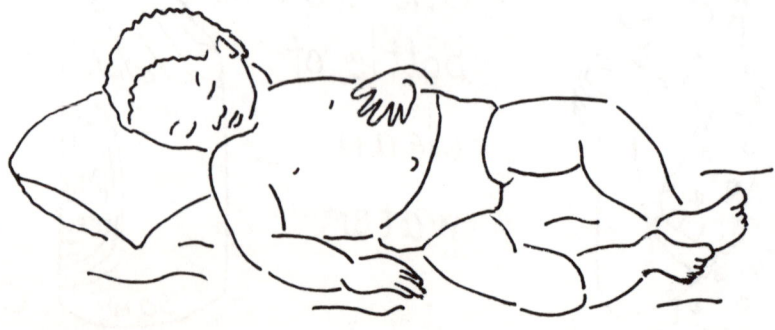

Leave blankets off a child with a fever

Give aspirin tablets:
2 tablets for anyone over 12 years
1 tablet for anyone from 6 to 12 years
½ tablet for anyone from 3 to 6 years
¼ tablet for anyone under 3 years
No aspirin for babies under 1 year
Give the child lots of liquids to drink: water; Special Rehydration Drink; tea or orange squash. If the fever is not better in a day, take the child to the clinic.

Colds and 'flu

These illnesses cause runny noses, sore throats, headaches and sometimes a fever. Colds and 'flu always go away in a few days without any medicine. Drinking plenty of water and other drinks will help. Rest as much as possible to give the body a chance to fight off the disease. Aspirin tablets will help the aches and pains and the fever.

Colds and 'flu do not come from getting cold or wet. A cold is caught from someone else who has one. They breathe the germs out of their mouths onto other people. If you have a cold try not to give it to other people, especially babies and old people. People catch colds more easily if they do not eat enough or sleep enough. If an adult or child is weak before they catch a cold, then it may turn into **bronchitis** or **pneumonia**. These are both dangerous diseases of the lungs. Go to a clinic if the cold or 'flu is getting much worse. Injections never help colds or 'flu.

Coughs

Coughs can be caused by many diseases. Usually a cough is not dangerous and will go away in a few days. Drinking lots of water will help. To make some cough medicine, squeeze a lemon and mix the juice with a little hot water and a spoonful of honey or sugar. Sip it slowly.

Guava and gum cough mixture

12 Gum tree leaves
12 Guava leaves
8 teaspoons or bottle-tops of sugar — preferably brown
1 family-sized (720 ml) fizzy-drink bottle of water

1 Wash leaves well
2 Put leaves, sugar and water in a cooking pan.
3 Boil for 15 minutes
4 Remove leaves and allow to cool.
5 Pour into a clean bottle and keep in a cool, dark place.

Give children 1 to 2 teaspoons of mixture 3 times a day. After a few days the mixture may go fizzy. Throw it away and make fresh mixture when needed.

Steam for a cough

Breathing over hot water helps soothe a cough. Put very hot water in a bucket. Place a towel or cloth over the head and breathe in the steam for 10 minutes. This will make breathing easier and lessen the cough. Be careful that children do not burn themselves with the hot water.

If there is a fever with the cough and it is painful to breathe, go to a clinic. Sitting near a smokey fire indoors is not good for coughs. Smoking cigarettes always makes coughs worse. Try to prevent young people from smoking. Once someone starts to smoke it is very hard for him to give up.

Pneumonia This is a disease of the lungs. Pneumonia is very dangerous in babies and small children. Diseases like 'flu, bronchitis, whooping cough and measles can turn into pneumonia.

Pneumonia starts with shivering and then a high fever. Sometimes very young babies have pneumonia with no fever. A child with pneumonia breathes very fast and his nostrils may be wide open. Often there are grunts or wheezing as he breathes and pain in the chest. If a sick child breathes more than 50 shallow breaths in one minute then he probably has pneumonia. The ribs may be pulled in as he breathes. Take him to a clinic quickly.

Whooping cough This starts like a cold with a runny nose, fever and cough. After about 2 weeks the 'whooping' starts. The child has a violent coughing attack and is unable to breathe in. Eventually he coughs up some **mucus** and there is a high sounding 'whoop' as the air rushes into the lungs. Then he may vomit.

Whooping cough can last for up to 4 months. The child may become very weak and malnourished. Small babies do not always 'whoop' but they may die because they cannot breathe or from malnutrition due to vomiting so often. Always take a baby who may have whooping cough to the clinic. Children with whooping cough need good feeding with lots of energy foods. Whooping cough can only be caught once by a child.

Prevent whooping cough by immunisation when babies are 3, 4 *and* 5 months old.

Mumps   Mumps starts 2 or 3 weeks after being near someone with the disease. There is a fever, and eating or opening the mouth is painful. After 2 days there is a soft swelling below the ears and under the jaw. Sometimes it only appears on one side. During this time it is difficult to eat but the child should be encouraged to eat soft, high-energy foods such as avocado pears and porridge with jam or margarine. The swelling goes away after about 10 days. Treat the fever and pain with aspirin.

The testicles of men and boys over 11 years old may swell up painfully. Women's breasts may be tender and swollen. The pain and swelling can be reduced with ice or wet cloths and by lying quietly. Mumps can be caught only once.

Worms   Worms get into many children. There are different kinds of worms. In the child's belly they multiply and make the child weak. Sometimes the worms may come out in the child's faeces which shows that there will be more inside. Some worms do not come out. They just make a child weak, pale and sick. The worms eat the food inside the child's gut. If a child's eyelids and tongue are very pale, she may have **anaemia**. This means the blood is losing its strength. Worms can cause anaemia.

Worms can be prevented. They are spread by animals and faeces on the ground. Always use a toilet or latrine and wash the hands afterwards.

If you think a child has worms take him to the clinic for medicine to kill them.

Tapeworms   can grow up to several metres long in the gut. White pieces of the worm may break off and be seen in the faeces. People can catch tapeworms in two ways: either by eating pig or cow meat that has not been properly cooked and contains tapeworm eggs; or by the tapeworm eggs coming out in faeces and being picked up by other people because the person does not use a latrine or toilet, and does not wash his hands. Tapeworm is dangerous if the baby worms get into the brain. This can cause headaches, fits or even death.

Threadworms   are about 1 cm long, white and very thin. They lay thousands of eggs on the outside of the **anus**. This causes itching especially at night when the threadworms come out. When the child scratches his anus he picks up the eggs on his fingers and under his finger nails. He might then pass the worm eggs to someone else on food or eat the eggs himself. Threadworms can sometimes be seen in the faeces. They are not dangerous but they are easily prevented by washing hands before eating.

If a child has threadworm keep his fingernails short and try to stop him scratching his bottom. Medicine from a clinic will kill the worms.

Hookworms
: are so small that they are not usually seen in faeces. They live in the gut and make a person weak and anaemic. Hookworm eggs come out in faeces and then hatch in damp soil. The young hookworms enter a person's body through bare feet so wearing shoes prevents hookworm.

    Hookworm can be treated with medicine from the clinic. Anaemia is treated by eating food such as meat, liver, eggs and chicken. Beans, peas, lentils and dark leafy vegetables also help anaemia.

Roundworms
: are pink or white and about 20 to 30 cm long. The eggs are spread from one person's faeces to another person's mouth if a latrine or toilet is not used. The young worms live in the blood and then move to the lungs. When they are coughed up they go into the gut where they grow into adults. They cause weakness and swollen bellies. Medicine from the clinic will kill roundworm. Prevent them by using latrines and washing hands and food before eating.

Paw-paw worm mixture
: 3 teaspoons of white juice from the stem or green fruit of the paw-paw tree
3 teaspoons of honey
1 cup of hot water.
Mix these together and drink. Drink a **laxative** with this and the dead worms will come out quicker.

Guineaworm
: larvae live in tiny water-flies in wells, ponds and shallow rivers. If someone drinks this water the larvae grow into long thin worms inside the body. After 9 to 18 months the female worm moves to the feet, ankles or hands. This causes vomiting, diarrhoea, **giddiness** and sometimes fainting. A few hours later the worm can be seen under the skin. When the skin is under water the worm lays her eggs. The worm comes out of the body when the eggs are all finished. She may be up to one metre long. If the worm is cut or broken it may cause blood poisoning. Wind the worm onto a small stick and pull it out slowly over about a week.

    Prevent guineaworm by protecting wells and drinking water so that people cannot stand in the water and waste water does not flow back in. Boil drinking water or strain through layers of fine cloth to catch the water-flies. Medicine from the clinic will kill any worms that are still inside the body.

Skin problems   Skin problems can be prevented by washing every day. The two most common skin problems in children are scabies and ringworm.

Scabies   are very small animals that make tunnels under the skin. They cannot be seen with the eyes. Scabies go between the fingers and toes, around the waist and on the **genitals** of boys and girls. Scabies make small, itchy sores. If a child scratches them a lot of the sores can become infected making sores with pus. Scabies can be caught by touching other children with them or from bedding and clothes that have been used by someone with scabies. If children are washed every day with soap and hot water and their blankets are put in the sun to air, they will not catch scabies.

Clinics have special medicine for treating scabies. All the family must be treated together or they will give scabies to each other again. Clothes and blankets must be washed well and hung in the sun to dry.

Ringworm   is not a worm. It appears as a patch of dry, itchy skin which spreads outwards in a ring. If the ringworm is in the hair then the hair will fall out. Adults rarely have ringworm. Children catch it easily from each other. Washing with soap and water will help prevent it and sometimes cures it too. Clinics have special cream for treating ringworm.

Chickenpox   starts 2 or 3 weeks after touching another child with the disease. Small, red, itchy spots appear on the body and then spread to the face, arms and legs. A small **blister** appears on the top of each spot. **Scabs** form when the blisters break. Once the scabs have formed the disease is not catching. There is usually a mild fever and the child feels unwell for a few days. Chickenpox can be caught only during the first week. It is not a dangerous disease. Finger nails should be cut short to prevent the child scratching the tops off the spots and causing infection. Put **gentian violet** on any infected spots.

To soothe the itching, bathe the child in warm water mixed with a handful of ground oatmeal, or boil some oatmeal in water, soak cloths in the mixture and lay them on the itching parts of the body. **Calamine lotion** on the spots will help the itching too.

Ticks   can appear on any part of the skin of a child, especially behind the ears. Look for them every day and if there is one do not pull it off: you may leave behind its head which could cause an infection. Hold a lighted cigarette near it or put petroleum jelly over it. Both of these will make it let go. Sometimes ticks cause Tick Bite Fever. This is a high fever and bad headaches. Go to a clinic for treatment.

Impetigo — causes sores with yellow scabs that spread across the face. It is very catching so any child with sores on his face should visit a clinic. Gentian violet will help dry up the sores. Washing every day with soap and water prevents impetigo. The germs are spread on hands or on towels and face cloths.

Petroleum jelly — causes rashes on some babies. Petroleum jelly is too thick and greasy for their delicate soft skin. Petroleum jelly is only suitable for babies bottoms. Use baby oil on their faces and bodies.

Malaria — Malaria is very common in many parts of Africa. There is no malaria in mountains; the weather is too cold for the malaria germs to grow. In big towns and cities where all the mosquitoes have been killed there is no malaria. If someone from a city goes into the rural areas, he may easily catch malaria because he has no immunity.

Malaria causes a high fever and headaches. Malaria in the brain can kill a child or damage the brain so he is always slow and dull. Children and adults, especially pregnant women, may catch malaria at any time. Malaria is especially bad during the rainy season when the mosquitoes are breeding. Children catch malaria more often between the ages of three months and five years. After that a child may have some immunity. The child can still catch malaria but it will not be so serious.

Malaria comes from mosquitoes. They suck the blood of someone who has the disease and then put the germs into the next person they bite. Mosquitoes breed in still water. They lay their eggs in pots, tins, barrels, ponds, puddles or maize leaves: anywhere they can find some water. The eggs hatch into larvae and after a few days the larvae come out of the water and fly away — to look for a person to bite.

Mosquitoes only come out when it is dark. During the day they stay in long grass or dark corners. Keep grass around the home cut short — this will keep snakes away too. Remove old pots or tins that could hold water. Mosquitoes can breed in only a cup of water. Rain barrels should be covered with a net or thin cloth to prevent mosquitoes from breeding in them. Fill ponds with earth unless they are really needed.

Babies should have a net or thin cloth over their cots so they are not bitten in the night. Close all bedroom windows before sunset. If possible, spray the bedroom with insect killer half an hour before going to bed.

When a child has mosquito bites he will scratch often. The bites can easily become infected and pus will form in them. Keep children's finger nails cut short and their hands clean. This prevents the tops of the mosquito bites being scratched off and germs getting into the bite. Put gentian violet on any infected bites. Calamine lotion stops bites from itching.

If a child has a high fever or many mosquito bites with pus, take him to the clinic. Children who live in urban areas should take **chloroquine** tablets when they visit the rural areas. Chloroquine treats and prevents malaria.

Bilharzia   This disease takes a long time to affect a person. Bilharzia is caused by a very small worm, or larva, which lays eggs in a person's **bladder**. If the person then passes urine into a stream or river the eggs will come out. They will hatch into larvae and then go into the body of a small snail. The larvae breed inside the snail and then go back into the river. If another person swims or walks in the river, the larvae will go through the skin and into his blood. When the larvae reaches the bladder they will lay more eggs. Some of the larvae may go into other parts of the body and make the person sick.

The first sign of bilharzia is blood in the urine. If bilharzia is not treated it can cause damage to many of the parts of the body including the brain. People with bilharzia feel tired and sick all the time. Anyone with blood in his urine should visit a clinic.

Bilharzia can be prevented by teaching children not to pass urine into streams and rivers. The children should try not to swim or play in rivers. If water with bilharzia is left in a pot for a whole day then the bilharzia will die. Bilharzia is also killed by boiling.

1 Person with bilharzia urinates in stream.
2 Urine has worm eggs in it.
3 Worm eggs go into snails.
4 Bilharzia worms come out of snail. They are so small you cannot see them
5 Person bathes or swims in stream. Bilharzia worms enter his body. through his skin.

Snail (real size)

Bilharzia cycle

Measles   Measles begins 10 days after being near another child with the disease. Measles starts like a cold: fever, runny nose, cough and red, sore eyes. After 2 or 3 days spots appear inside the mouth. The tiny white spots look like grains of salt. One or two days later a rash appears, first on the neck. It then spreads to the face and body and then the arms and legs. The child is very unhappy, with diarrhoea and sometimes vomiting. If the mouth is very sore the child will not want to eat and may become malnourished. Help the child to eat soft, high-energy foods. Babies should be breast-fed often. Give plenty to drink and use Special Rehydration Drink if there is fever or diarrhoea. Fresh orange juice helps to keep sore mouths clean.

The rash lasts about 5 days and then the child begins to feel better. Measles kills many children every year, especially malnourished children. Measles can lead to pneumonia, blindness or diarrhoea that lasts a long time. To prevent blindness make sure that children eat orange coloured fruits such as mangoes, carrots and apricots and ox liver or whole fish.

Keep children with measles well away from other children and do not allow visitors. Breast-fed babies under 9 months are usually protected from measles. Measles can be prevented in everyone by one injection given at the children's clinic at 9 months of age.

Polio   Polio starts like 'flu with a fever and a stiff neck. Most children then get better. But sometimes part of the body becomes weak or stops working. This is usually one or both legs. If the breathing or swallowing muscles stop working then the child will die. Once the muscles stop working there is no medicine which will cure the **paralysis**.

A child with polio should stay in bed and keep away from other children for at least two weeks. Injections must *never* be given to a child who may have polio. Any injection can cause paralysis. The child should eat plenty of good food.

A child with paralysis from polio may learn to walk again but only if he is helped soon. He needs exercises to build up the strength in the good muscles. His arms or legs will go stiff if they are not exercised often. Some strength may return during the first year.

Polio happens more often to children between one and five years. Breast-feeding will protect babies for the first few months. If all babies are immunised with drops at 3, 4 *and* 5 months then the disease would disappear.

Tetanus   Tetanus germs grow in dirty cuts and wounds. The germs produce a strong poison. When this poison gets into the blood it makes the body go stiff and tight. At first the child cannot open his mouth and then the rest of his body tightens up. This causes great pain. The child dies of

malnutrition and **exhaustion**. Anyone with tetanus needs hospital treatment.

New-born babies can catch tetanus if their umblical cord is cut with a dirty knife or if it is not kept clean.

Tetanus can be prevented by washing all cuts and wounds carefully. Always go to the clinic for treatment for large or deep wounds.

Immunisation at 3, 4 *and* 5 months and again *every* 5 years will protect against tetanus. Pregnant mothers should be immunised to protect their new-born babies.

Diptheria This starts, like a cold with a cough, fever and headache. A grey skin grows over the back of the throat and nose. This may stop the child from breathing. Diptheria is easily spread and a very dangerous disease. It must always be treated in hospital. If a child does not die from diptheria he may always have a weak heart. Diptheria can be prevented with immunisation at 3, 4 *and* 5 months and at 5 years.

Tuberculosis

Tuberculosis, or TB, is a long lasting and easily spread disease of the lungs. Malnourished or weak people catch TB more than healthy, well-fed people. If anyone in the home has TB then the rest of the family will easily catch it too.

The signs of TB are a long lasting cough, weakness and loss of weight and sometimes pain in the chest or back. If the TB is serious then blood may be coughed up. TB can also affect the brain and bones of children.

Children who eat well and live in clean, dry homes are not so likely to catch TB. Immunisation at birth and again at 5 years will protect against TB for life.

If a child is sick, do not allow him to sleep in the same bed with other children. If possible, put him in a separate room. Sick adults should sleep separately too. Do not allow sick people near babies, small children or old people.

Sick people should use separate cups and plates at meals. They should use separate towels and face-cloths for washing.

Questions

1. What food will help a sick child get better quickly?
2. What causes diarrhoea?
3. What are the signs of dehydration? How can dehydration be prevented and treated?
4. Imagine your sister has a cold. How will you make her feel better?
5. How do children catch worms? How can worms be prevented?
6. What is malaria? Where does it come from? How can it be prevented?
7. What causes bilharzia? How can we prevent it?
8. How can you help a child with polio?

Activities

1. Make some Special Rehydration Drink. Taste it. Show your family how to make it. Tell them when to use it.
2. Write a story about a boy with diarrhoea. How did he catch it? How did he get better?
3. Make some cough mixture. Give it to someone with a cough. Show them how to breathe steam from hot water.
4. Draw a poster telling people about worms and how they can be prevented.
5. Act out different signs of sickness. See if other children can guess what disease you have.
6. Make a poster showing signs of sickness to watch for in babies and children.
7. Draw a picture of your local clinic. How many people work there? Find out how many children and adults they treat every week. What are the most common diseases they treat?

8 Making our lives safer

Accidents in the home

If everybody takes care to prevent accidents then they need not happen. One cannot help being stung by a bee; but children can be taught not to play near a bees' nest.

Most accidents happen in the home. Homes can be very dangerous.

Burns No one should play near fires because they will easily be burnt. Try not to have the cooking fire on the ground. A cooking stove above a child's reach is best. An open cooking fire on a raised mound of clay will help. Turn handles of cooking pans inwards so that small children cannot reach them and knock them over. Always pick up cooking pans using a cloth — the handle may be very hot. It may either burn the hand or cause the pan to be dropped and spill boiling food all over the person.

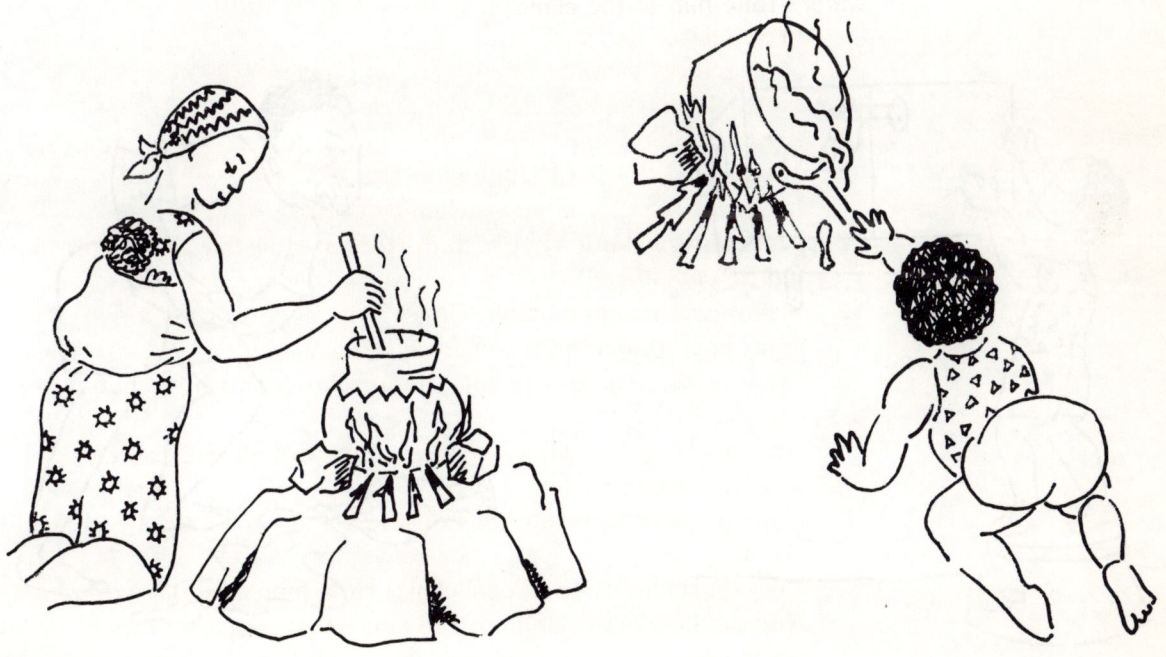

Build a cooking fire above the ground...   *... to prevent this happening.*

Keep lamps and matches where children cannot reach them. Never allow children to play with matches. They must learn that matches are for adults only.

If someone is burned, put the burned part into cold water *quickly*. Keep it there for ten minutes or longer. If the burn is large put the whole body into clean, cold water; either a bath or a river. If the skin falls off take the person to the clinic quickly. Cover the burn with a *clean* cloth. Do not remove their clothes. Give the person warm, sweet drinks and keep him wrapped in warm clothes or a blanket. Small burns are best left uncovered. Never rub oil, margarine or grease into burns.

Poison Many children die from swallowing things that are poisonous. The most common poisons that children eat are those that are found in the home. These are rat poisons, medicines, bleach and detergents, matches, cigarettes, paraffin and petrol. All these things should be kept well away from children. They should be in a locked cupboard. *Never* keep paraffin, petrol or other poisonous liquids in sweet fizzy drink or beer bottles. Children or even adults may drink them. Children should be taught which leaves and berries are poisonous in their area.

If someone has drunk poison, make him vomit. Put your finger down his throat. Make him drink water with soap or salt in it. Give the child milk, with beaten eggs or flour mixed with the water. Keep making him vomit until the vomit is clear. Do *not* make a person vomit if he has drunk paraffin, petrol or acids. Make him drink lots of milk or flour and water. Take him to the clinic.

Keep poisons and medicines locked up

NEVER put paraffin in sweet fizzy drink bottles

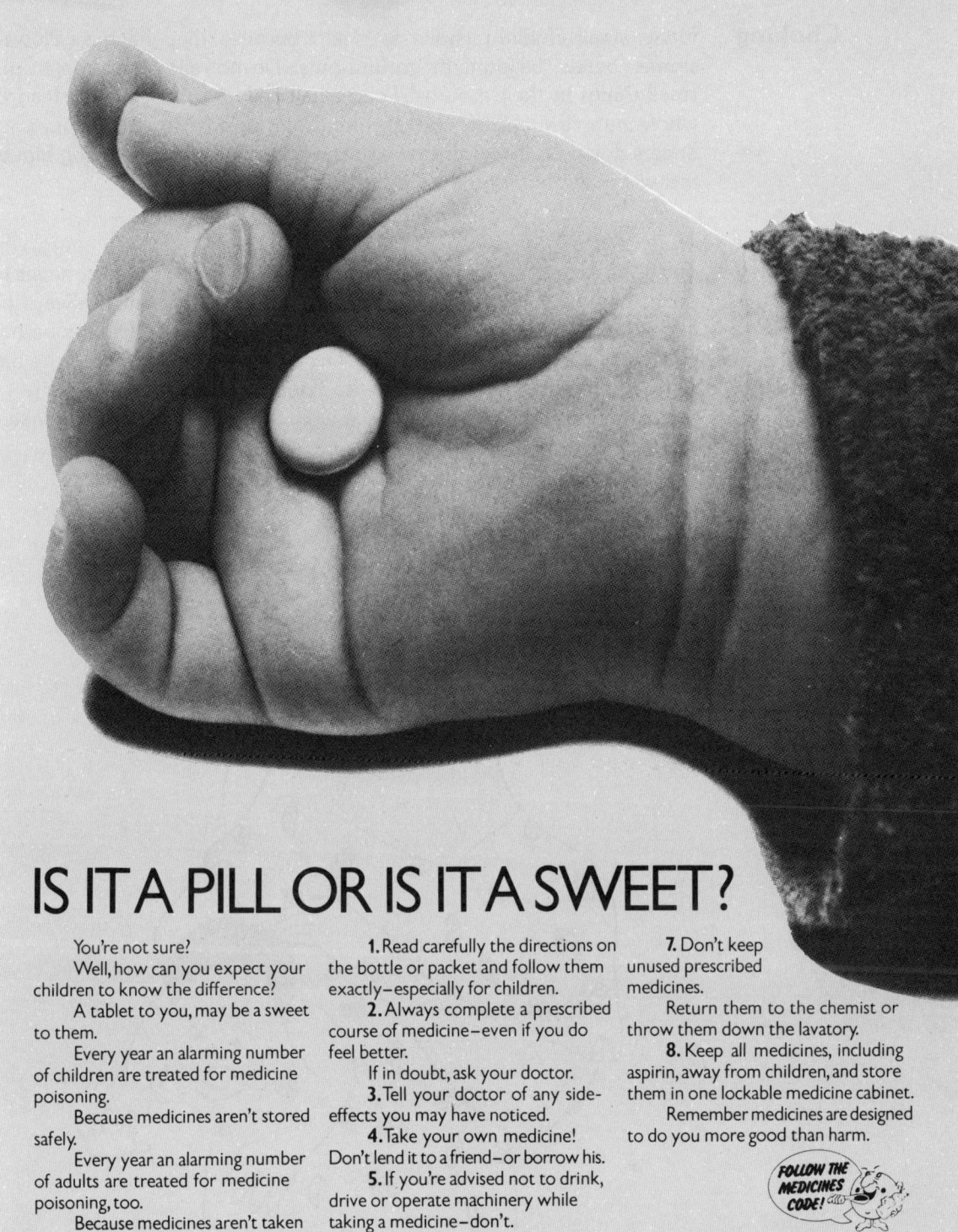

IS IT A PILL OR IS IT A SWEET?

You're not sure?
Well, how can you expect your children to know the difference?
A tablet to you, may be a sweet to them.
Every year an alarming number of children are treated for medicine poisoning.
Because medicines aren't stored safely.
Every year an alarming number of adults are treated for medicine poisoning, too.
Because medicines aren't taken seriously enough.
Always follow this Medicine Code.

1. Read carefully the directions on the bottle or packet and follow them exactly—especially for children.
2. Always complete a prescribed course of medicine—even if you do feel better.
If in doubt, ask your doctor.
3. Tell your doctor of any side-effects you may have noticed.
4. Take your own medicine! Don't lend it to a friend—or borrow his.
5. If you're advised not to drink, drive or operate machinery while taking a medicine—don't.
6. If you're pregnant ask your doctor about any medicines you take.

7. Don't keep unused prescribed medicines.
Return them to the chemist or throw them down the lavatory.
8. Keep all medicines, including aspirin, away from children, and store them in one lockable medicine cabinet.
Remember medicines are designed to do you more good than harm.

FOLLOW THE MEDICINES CODE!

The Health Education Council
Helping you to better health.

Advice on using and storing medicines (produced by the British Health Education Council)

Choking Many small children choke to death because they have swallowed stones, beads, balloons or ground-nuts. Do not allow children to put small things in their mouths. Feed small children nut butter instead of whole nuts. If a child is choking, hold him upside down and put your fingers down his throat. Either you can hook out what is choking him or this will make him vomit it up.

Electricity This is very dangerous if children play with it. Teach children never to poke things into electric sockets. Plugs and switches must always be turned off. Fraying or ragged wires should be replaced. If someone has an electric shock, turn off the electricity *before you touch him*. If he has stopped breathing then give him the **Kiss of Life** (see pp 76–77).

Look around your home and see what things can be done to make it safer for the whole family.

A choking baby

Accidents outside

Places where there are machines are dangerous for children. Electric saws and grinding mills can kill or disable children. Machines and tools must *always* be locked up so that children cannot play with them.

Snakes   Snakes live in long grass. Keep grass around the home short and keep creepers off the house. Do not lift up logs or stones without first looking underneath as well as you can. Most snakes do not bite unless they are attacked. They usually go away before you see them.

If someones is bitten by a snake do not move him. Moving a person helps to spread the poison around the body. Keep him calm. Cover him with a blanket to keep him warm. Get help quickly. If possible take the dead snake with you to the clinic then the health workers will know how to treat the snake bite. Do *not* tie anything around the arm or leg which is bitten. This can do more harm than the bite because it stops the blood from running.

Dog bites   These should always be treated at a clinic, however small. Dogs that bite may have **rabies**. Rabies is a serious disease that kills people very painfully if they are not treated quickly. The dog must be locked up to see if it has rabies. If it cannot be caught it must be killed.

Roads   Children (and some adults!) need to be taught how to use roads safely.

Walking   Whenever possible use a footpath or pavement. If you stop to talk to a friend keep to the side so that other people are not pushed into the road. Where there is no footpath keep close to the edge of the road. If traffic drives on the left, walk on the right. If traffic drives on the right, then walk on the left. Never walk in the middle of the road. The road may look empty, but cars travel very fast. Do not stand in the road on sharp bends or in places where traffic cannot see walkers.

In towns always use the special crossing places. Less time is spent walking further along the road to the crossing then going to hospital after an accident! Look both to the left and to the right *twice* before crossing. Keep on the edge of the road until it is clear. Do not stand half way across the road waiting for traffic to pass.

If there is no special crossing do not cross the road on a corner or from behind a vehicle; you cannot see traffic and it cannot see you. Walk straight across the road; do not run or wander slowly.

Children should set off for school in good time so that they do not have to take dangerous risks by hurrying.

Keep dogs on a lead or string when they are on the road. Many

serious accidents are caused by dogs running into the road in front of cars.

When herding cattle, sheep or goats on the road there must be someone at the front with a red cloth tied to a stick, and someone at the back.

Children should never play on or near a road. Ball games are especially dangerous as a child may chase the ball across the road in front of a car.

Cycling

Cyclists as well as car drivers should learn the Highway Code and road laws. Cyclists are in special danger because they share the road with large, fast vehicles. Bicycles have no protection and cannot easily be seen by buses and lorries.

Always use the special cycle track if there is one, or keep to the edge of the road. In slow moving traffic do not 'weave' in and out of other vehicles. They may move without having seen you.

Be careful not to ride into people walking or children playing. Even a bicycle can cause a broken arm or leg.

Make sure that the bicycle is in good working order. There should be good brakes on both back and front wheels. Tyres must be pumped up hard. Never ride a bicycle that is too big: the feet must touch the ground on both sides when sitting on the saddle. Do not overload the bicycle with so much luggage that it cannot be controlled or may tip over.

Never ride at night without a good light on the front *and* the back of the bicycle. A cyclist may be able to see cars coming, but they cannot see the cyclist until it is too late. When walking or cycling at night always wear a white or pale coloured shirt or dress. Drivers cannot see dark clothes. If you have no light clothes then fix a page of newspaper to your back and front. This may look funny but it could save your life.

If someone has a car accident, or falls out of a tree, do not move him. Cover him with a blanket or coat and keep him warm. Get help quickly. Children often fall out of trees, especially during the mango season! Trees that have dead branches are especially dangerous. If a child falls out of a tree get help before moving him. If any bones are broken moving him may make it worse. If an arm or leg is bleeding very badly tie a sock or a neck-tie around the limb just above the wound to stop the bleeding. This should only be done if there is a lot of blood and the tie must be loosened every 30 minutes.

Climb trees carefully!

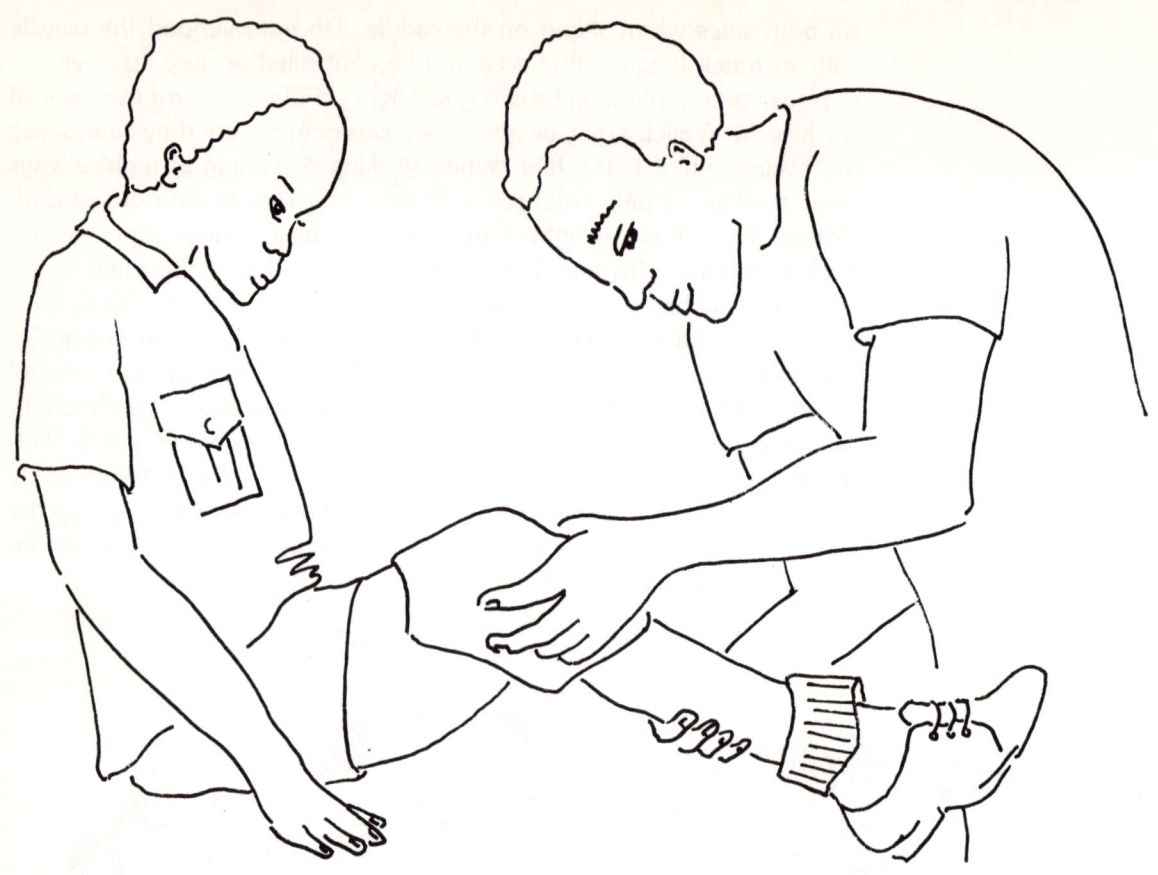

Use clean bandages for cuts

Cuts and wounds Cuts should be washed with soap and water which has been boiled and then cooled. Do not use a bandage unless it is *very clean*. Deep or large cuts must be treated at a clinic. If a cut or wound becomes hot, red or swollen, smells bad or has pus in it then go to a clinic.

Water Children can drown in very shallow water. Do not allow children to play near wells, streams, the sea or rivers on their own. Wells should always have a strong cover over them. Even a child who can swim well can drown in a river. If a child, or adult, looks as if she is drowning, get her out of the water quickly. Make sure there is nothing in her mouth. Remove false teeth from adults' mouths. Lay her on her back and tilt her head backwards so that her mouth falls open. Hold her nose closed with your fingers. Put your mouth over her mouth and breathe air into her lungs. Do this until she starts to breathe again by herself.

If a baby has stopped breathing only blow a little air into her lungs. Too much air will burst her lungs.

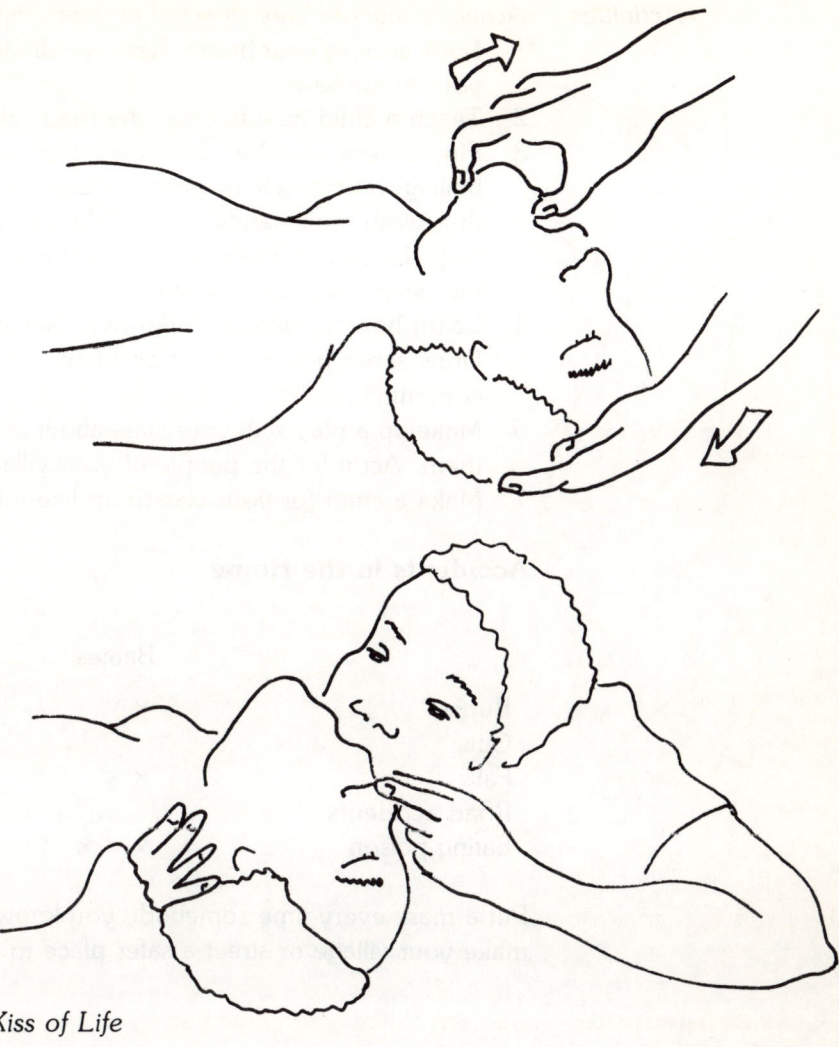

Kiss of Life

Shock

Accidents can cause **shock** in a child or adult. This makes them very cold and faint. If a person faints, put his head between his knees until he feels better. To treat and prevent shock, cover the person with a coat or blanket. Give him sips of warm tea or milk with sugar in it.

Questions for pupils
1. What should you do if someone is burnt in a fire?
2. What rules should a cyclist learn?
3. How many different accidents could happen in the home?
4. Where do snakes live?
5. How should a cut be treated?
6. What poisons should be locked up in the home?

Activities *Activities marked* are directed at older children and teachers.*
1. Look around your home. Remove all the dangerous things to make your home safer.
2. Teach a child how to cross the road safely.*
3. Find a piece of cotton cloth about the size of a handkerchief. Put it in boiling water to kill the germs. Hang the cloth in the sun. When it is dry, wash your hands and put the cloth in a clean plastic or paper bag. Keep in in a safe place.. use it to cover cuts or burns. When it has been used, boil it again.*
4. Learn how to swim and life-save. Never swim on your own.
5. Draw some posters about accidents. Stick them on a wall in your community.
6. Make up a play with your class about accidents and how to prevent them. Act it for the people of your village or street.
7. Make a chart for your classroom like this:

Accidents in the Home

	Babies	Children	Adults
Burns	x	x x	x
Cuts		x x x	x x
Falls	x x	x x	x
Road accidents		x	x x x
Eating poison	x x x	x	x x x

Put a mark every time somebody you know has an accident. Can you make your village or street a safer place to live in?

9 Playing with children

Children need to play. A child who plays a lot will learn more quickly when he goes to school. Good food and health care make children grow into strong adults. But they also need their minds to be stretched by playing with toys and other children. Children who sit with nothing to do and no one to play with will find school work and learning more difficult than children who are always playing and interested in the people and things around them. Children need to grow up in a place where they are encouraged to find out more. They need a home where they can enjoy learning and testing out new skills.

Toys and friends help children to play. They need to be helped in their play; children cannot always think of all the games on their own. Playing teaches children how to use their bodies and their brains.

Learning to use hands and eyes together

79

Playing with babies

Sing and talk to babies and young children. Tell them stories, even if they cannot talk yet. They will learn by listening to you. When talking to babies let them talk back to you. The funny noises they make are their way of talking. The more you talk to a baby the happier she will be. Bathe her in words and she will learn to respond to people and to speak well.

Babies like toys that make a noise. To make a rattle put some stones or large seeds into a plastic bottle or tin. A wooden spoon and a tin plate make a good noise. Make sure the toys are safe for a baby. Check that she cannot open the bottle or tin and swallow the seeds.

Thread some cotton reels on a string for a baby to feel and suck. Babies learn a lot about the shape and feel of things with their mouths. Make sure their toys are always clean and cannot cut their mouths or fingers.

Young babies learn by being touched and watching things. Babies like being carried on their mothers' backs. They can feel the warmth and security of their mothers and they can see everything around them. A baby will not learn anything if she is unhappy or feels unloved.

Babies enjoy games like 'Peek-a-boo' — hiding behind your hand or a tree and then suddenly appearing.

Make a **mobile** for a baby to watch. Hang interesting things from a stick: leaves; flowers; bottle tops; coloured paper shapes. Hang it where the air will make it move slowly around.

Even the smallest babies love bathing. At first they like the feel of splashing in the water. When they can pick things up they will quickly learn about pouring.

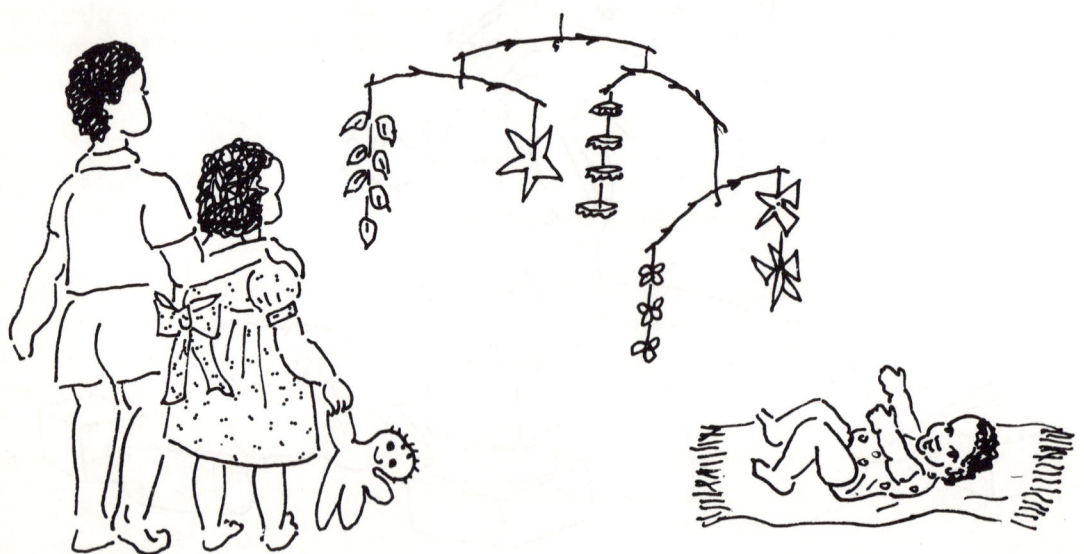

Watching a mobile

Pre-school playgroups

Children over 3 years old always enjoy going to a pre-school playgroup. A playgroup is a place with toys and games and adults who will help children want to play and do things. Children are helped to develop their minds and bodies. They learn to play with and talk to children of their own age and to be away from their parents for a few hours. This will make it easier for them when they start school. They will learn about colours, sizes, cutting, counting and many games. They will learn about washing, painting and perhaps they will grow vegetables.

If there is no playgroup near you, could some mothers start one? There are short courses where mothers can learn how to be playgroup leaders. Most playgroups are run by local mothers. Sometimes fathers help too. School-children can help run the playgroup during the holidays. By helping in a playgroup children will learn to be better parents when they grow up.

Some playgroups cook a balanced meal for the children. This teaches the children about food and also the dangers of touching hot cookng pans or going too near fires. After the meal the children learn how to clean their teeth, using a chewed green stick. The children are checked every day by the playgroup leader to see if they are healthy.

Children learn a lot by pretending. They can pretend they are mothers and fathers, that they are going shopping or that they are going to work. Make them hats out of newspaper to help them pretend. Make a play skirt out of a plastic sack cut into strips round the hem. Thread bottle tops or seed pods on the ends of the strips to make it rattle. A child with poor clothes will feel more attractive and confident if she has flowers in her hair and round her neck while she is playing.

Children who have had a difficult time may want to play a game about it often. For example, Peter had been in hospital for a month. He wanted to play hospitals for several weeks after his return home. This helped to accept the experience.

Games and activities

Shops Playing shops teaches children how to give and take without fighting. They learn about numbers and about quantities of food and money. The 'shopkeeper' can put his things into piles of equal size. Empty food packets, jars, bottles or wild fruits can be 'bought' and 'sold'. Bottle tops, leaves, stones, seeds or paper can be used as money. If it is a food shop the children can learn which are good, healthy foods. Children learn how to take turns and be polite to each other.

Clinics Some playgroups have a 'clinic'. One child is the nurse and the other children and their dolls are the patients. A play clinic helps to take away the fear of visiting a real clinic when children are ill or need to be immunised.

A play clinic should never have old medicine bottles for the children to play with. The children may think of them as toys and if they find a medicine bottle at home they might play with it and drink from it. Even clean, washed medicine bottles are dangerous. Empty medicine bottles should only be used for teaching children they are dangerous and that only adults must touch them.

At a play clinic, a stick can be used for a thermometer and a squash bottle for medicine. Clean rags make good 'bandages'.

Dolls

Playing with a doll will teach a child how to care for and love someone else. Both boys and girls like playing with dolls. Boys will be better fathers if they know how to love and care for other people. You can make a doll with an old sock. Stuff it with dried grass or paper. Sew a happy face on it. Make a little baby carrier so that the doll can be carried on the child's back when he is not playing with it.

How to make a rag doll

You will need:

30 cm of fabric
sewing thread to match
contrasting thread for face
wool for hair
scissors, pins, newspaper
needle
scraps of fabric, cotton from fields or dried grass for stuffing
pieces of different fabric or wool for clothes.

1. Copy the pattern onto newspaper with a pencil and ruler. Cut out two bodies, two arms and two legs. (see fig 1)
2. Lay the pattern pieces onto the fabric as close together as possible. Pin.
3. Cut out the six pieces.
4. Fold arm pieces in half, inside out. Sew down the side and across the rounded end, leaving the straight end free. Turn to right side out.
5. Repeat with legs.
6. Stuff arms and legs with cut-up fabric scraps, cotton or grass.
7. Sew a smiling face on the head. Do not use buttons for eyes as they may come off and be swallowed by a child.
8. Pin body pieces together inside out.
9. Sew round body and head, leaving gaps at the side for arms and the bottom open. Turn right side out.
10. Stuff head tightly.
11. Sew in arms and stuff body tightly.

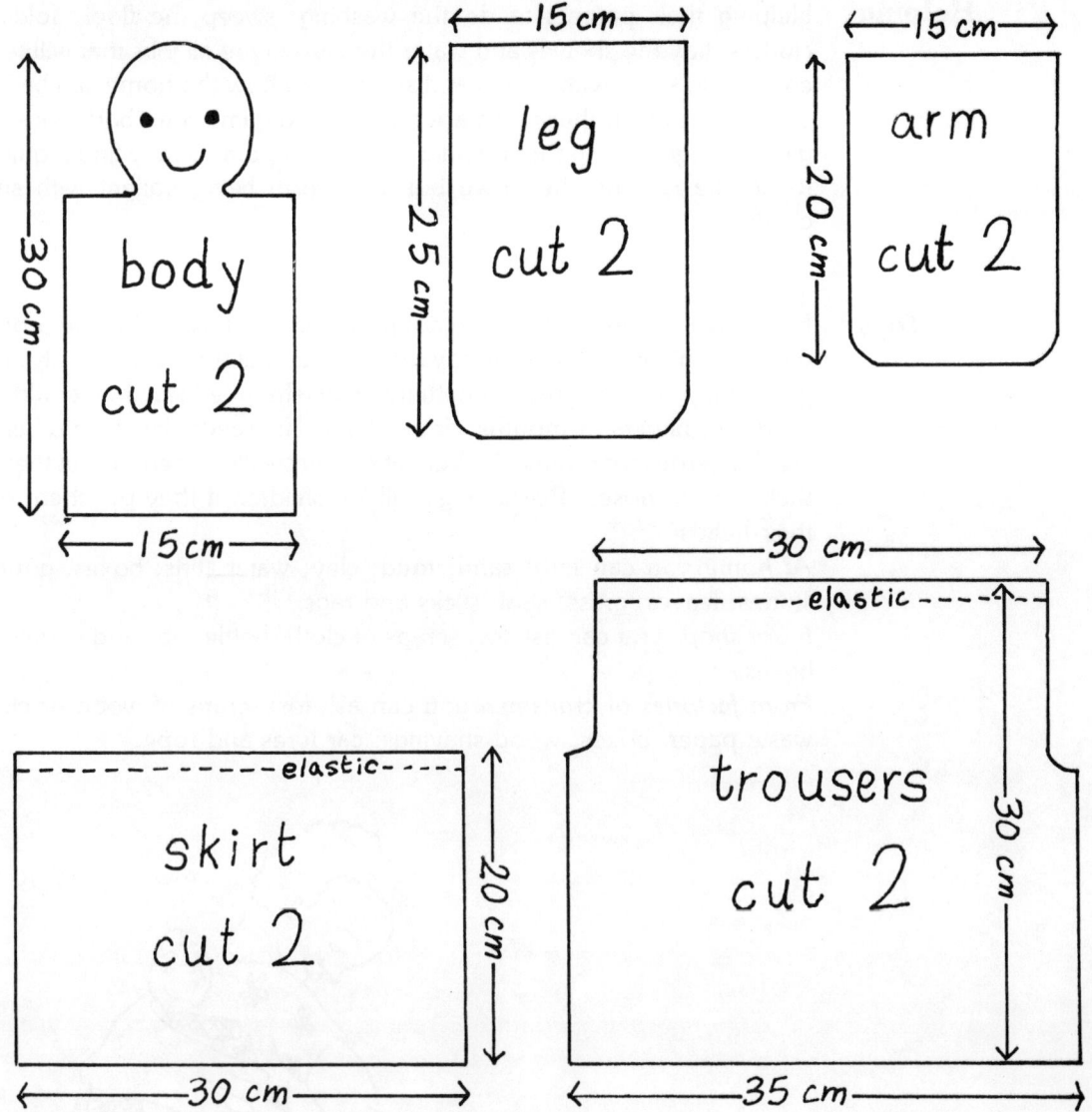

Fig 1: pattern for a rag doll

12 Sew in legs.
13 Sew wool on head for hair.
14 Make a dress or trousers for doll or knit a jumper with odd lengths of wool.

How to make a doll's baby carrier

Cut out a piece of fabric 30 cm by 30 cm and sew a hem round the edge. Sew four strips of fabric 50 cm by 10 cm into straps. Sew the straps onto the square.

Helping Helping their parents to do the washing, sweep the floor, fold the clothes, tidy the shelves and water the garden are all jobs that will teach children to work with others and show them how the home can be kept clean and tidy. If these jobs are treated as a game then both boys and girls will enjoy doing them. Older children or parents may find it quicker to do the jobs on their own but it is worth being patient with small children.

Toys Expensive toys from shops are not necessary. Nature and waste provide plenty of things to make into toys and games. All sorts of materials make good play things. Avoid anything with sharp edges that could cut children's fingers or mouths. Small things like seeds, beads and berries are dangerous for young children who may swallow them or put them in their ears or noses. Plastic bags will kill children if they put them over their heads.

At home you can find: sand; mud; clay; water; tins; boxes; gourds; stones; leaves; grass; sisal; sticks and rags.

From shops you can ask for: scraps of cloth; bottle tops and cardboard boxes.

From factories or craftsmen you can ask for: scraps of wood or cloth; waste paper; boxes; wood shavings; car tyres and rope.

Helping in the home

A large wooden or cardboard box can be great fun. Children will invent all kinds of different games. The box can be a boat, a bed, a car, a nest, a television or a cave.

Cars and trains can be made from blocks of wood with bottle tops or jam jar lids as wheels.

Home-made toys often last longer than plastic or shop-bought toys. If children make them then they will look after them carefully. Playing with toys helps children use their imagination and make the games they play more interesting.

Empty matchboxes and bits of wood from a carpenter make good building bricks; so do sawn-up loofah fruits. Children will spend hours making little houses and villages.

Clay

Help children make some farm animals and people out of clay. Young children can make fence posts and very young children enjoy the feel of sticky mud between their fingers and toes and can make simple mud pies. Bake the clay in the sun. If there is brick making in the area then the clay could be baked hard in a brick oven.

Making clay models is as much fun as playing with them later. Hands must be washed carefully after playing with clay or mud, otherwise worm eggs might be trapped under the finger nails and later eaten.

Pictures

Children love making pictures. Paint and crayons are expensive but glue is cheap and easy to make.

Mix one big spoonful of rice, maize or wheat flour with a large cup of water in a cooking pan. Cook it slowly, stirring all the time until it is thick. If a teaspoon of salt is added it will keep for a few days. Make a glue brush with a green stick. Beat or chew one end to make it 'hairy'. Use the glue and brush for sticking leaves, twigs, flower petals, sand and coloured paper onto newspaper, paper sacks or banana leaves. The children can make patterns or pictures of people, animals and homes. Small children will want to stick the leaves and petals anywhere, discovering for themselves about making pictures. This is an important way to learn.

Before sticking, the children can sort the petals into separate piles for each colour.

Paint can be made by grinding up old bricks, charcoal or dried flowers into a powder. Mix the powder with thin flour glue.

Looking at pictures helps children learn to read. At first a baby will hold the picture upside down and just look at the colours and shapes. Then she will learn that the shape of a ball or a man is the same as a real ball or man. At first babies cannot see that a real object that they know can be shown as a flat picture in a book. If they are shown lots of pictures, especially of faces and people, they will soon be able to name objects from a book.

Turning the pages of a book carefully is an important skill. Children should be taught that books are very precious and should be treated with great respect. If a young child learns this then she will look after books carefully all her life. Many books are ruined because children or adults crumple up or tear the pages or bend the covers back too far.

Learning to read helps the health of the family. If a mother can read she will learn about keeping her family clean, feeding her children well, and immunisations. Today's children are tomorrow's parents.

If there are no picture books they can be made by sticking greetings cards and pictures from old magazines together. Sew the cards together will string or strong thread. Stick pictures of things that children see around them onto the blank pages with flour glue.

If there is no paper children can draw pictures with a stick on the ground. Blackboard chalk is cheap. Draw pictures with chalk on the pavement or on walls or rocks. It is easily washed off.

Hearing stories is an important way for children to learn about their language, their history and their people. Every country has many folk tales and fables. Some of them have actions or songs that the children can join in. This helps to keep their attention and involve them in the story. Grandparents usually have a lot of good stories to tell children.

Bottle tops

Bottle tops have many uses and can be found outside most village shops or bottle stores. Children can sort them into different colours. Then they can count them. If a child can only count to 4 or 5 then she can put them in groups of that number. This helps her to learn about addition and multiplication by discovery. Understanding about numbers is needed before a child can learn to write numbers.

A child of 4 years should be able to hit a large nail with a hammer or a big stone. She can bang holes in the middle of the bottle tops. Then she can thread the bottle tops onto a piece of wire. This will make a good rattle. Bottle tops can be threaded onto string and tied round the legs for dancing.

Threading helps children to use their fingers, hands and eyes together to do small, difficult tasks. This is the first stage in learning to write.

Other things that can be threaded are cotton reels, leaves, beads, large seeds, lengths of bamboo or stalks, pieces of cardboard and pods. These can be threaded onto string, bark, sisal, wool or strong grass.

Size and shape

A collection of sticks, stones and seed pods can be sorted into different piles by children according to their size and shape. The small child will put them into piles of 'big' and 'small'. As she gets older she will learn the difference between fat and thin, long and short and round and square. Tins, boxes, bottle tops, sticks and leaves can also be used in this game.

Learning about shape and size is the first stage towards reading, writing and arithmetic.

Balancing Empty food tins also have many uses. A large tin can be balanced on the head. A little sand in the bottom of the tin will make it easier. Learning to balance things on the head is a useful skill.

Tins placed in a line on the ground are fun to walk along. Bury the bottoms in the ground so that they do not tip over. Put them close together for small children and further apart for older children. Logs, blocks of wood, stones or bricks can also be made into balancing paths. Make sure the tins have smooth edges at the top. Jagged tin can easily cut fingers.

Balancing

Water All children love playing with water. Fill a big bowl or bath with clean water. Provide some cups, a tin with holes in the bottom (but no sharp edges), big leaves, seed pods that float, hollow gourds and plastic bottles or anything that will not break or cut the children. Pawpaw and banana stems make good water pipes. Pieces of wood or seed pods can be boats. The same toys can also be played with in dry sand.

The Sun Playing with the sun is fun. Children can chase their shadows and draw around them on the ground. They can make the shadow of their fingers point at things and their shadows can dance with other children's shadows.

Balls There are many different games that can be played with balls. A football can be made from a strong plastic bag stuffed hard with paper or grass and tied tightly at both ends. It will not puncture, costs nothing and can be replaced if lost. Playing football teaches both boys and girls how to play well together, keep to the rules and accept victory for the other team.

'Blow Football' is a good game. Make a small ball out of paper. Find two or more sticks of bamboo, reed or plastic pipe about 10 cm long. Scratch a football pitch about 1 m long in the ground. Each side blows the ball with their sticks along the ground towards their goal.

Home-made football

Music Music is part of all children's lives. We all have voices to sing with. Musical instruments are expensive to buy but they are cheap to make. Use tins and plastic bags for drums. Big tins make low bangs and small tins make high bangs. Two pieces of wood or two tins can be banged together. Flatten a tin and attach it loosely to a stick for a cymbal. A cooking oil tin or petrol tin, some strong string or an elastic band and a length of wood can be used to make a guitar. Flatten some bottle tops with a hammer or a heavy stone and thread them onto wire to make a tambourine. Make a rattle using a tin or a gourd filled with stones or seeds and a stick for a handle.

Singing and dancing help children to use their bodies in time to the music. Singing and dancing in a group teaches them how to play together as a team. Songs help children to learn their language, or a new one. In countries where schoolwork is not in the home language songs will help children learn a little before they go to school.

Play area Is there a play area near your home? Make it safe by clearing away any rubbish, tins and broken bottles. Cut down any dead branches from the trees. Make a stepping path with logs or flat stones. Make a see-saw with a plank or long log over a forked tree trunk.

If you have enough car or tractor tyres put them upright in a line with their bottoms buried in the ground. Then children can crawl through them and climb over them. A blanket spread over them makes an exciting dark tunnel.

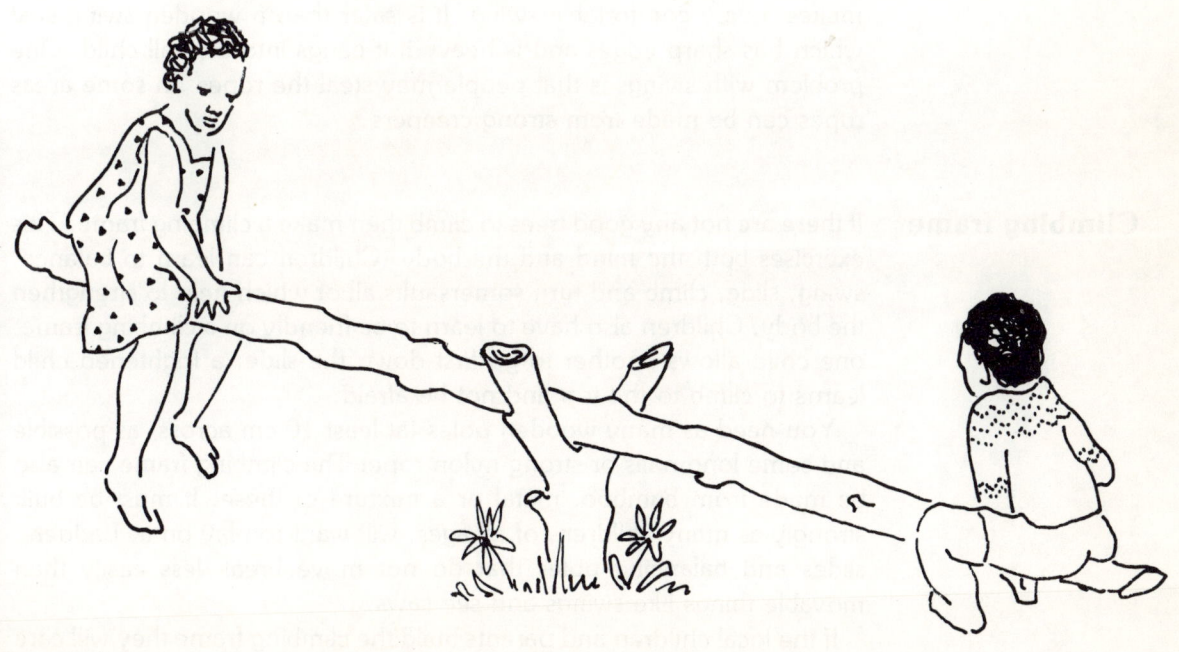

See-saw

Swinging

A car tyre cut and turned inside out and hung by a rope from a tree makes a very comfortable swing. It is safer than a wooden swing seat which has sharp edges and is heavy if it bangs into a small child. One problem with swings is that people may steal the ropes. In some areas ropes can be made from strong creepers.

Climbing frame If there are not any good trees to climb then make a climbing frame. This exercises both the mind and the body. Children can learn to balance, swing, slide, climb and turn somersaults all of which help to strengthen the body. Children also have to learn to be friendly on a climbing frame: one child allows another to go first down the slide; a frightened child learns to climb to the top and not be afraid.

You need as many wooden poles (at least 10 cm across) as possible and some long nails or strong nylon rope. The climbing frame can also be made from bamboo, metal or a mixture of these. It must be built strongly as many children, of all ages, will want to play on it. Ladders, slides and balancing poles that do not move break less easily than movable things like swings and see-saws.

If the local children and parents build the climbing frame they will care for it and protect it from **vandals** or people taking it for firewood.

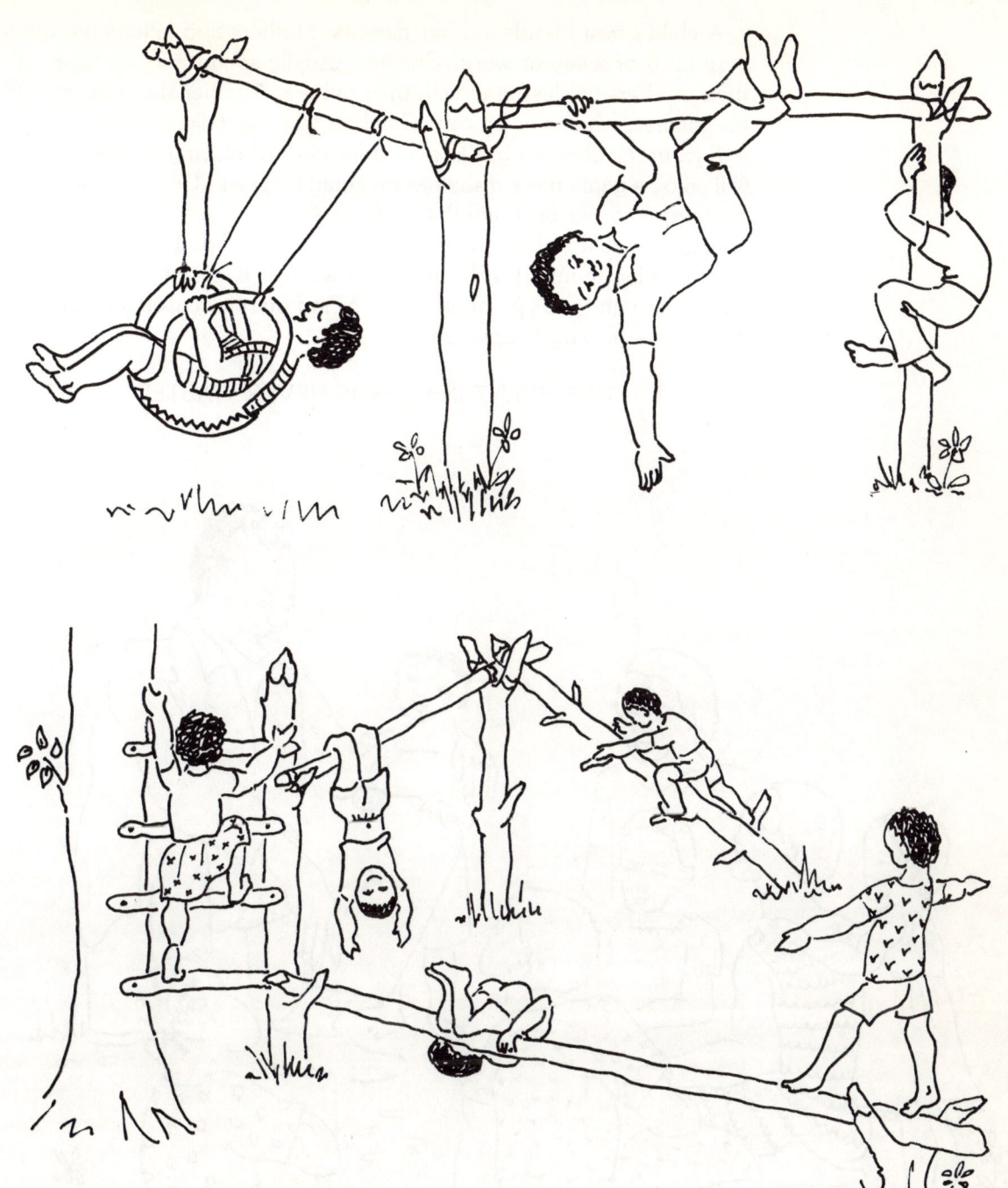

Climbing frames

A little house or platform made from poles and bamboo with a grass roof is an exciting place for children to play. It can be used for playing games of 'mothers and fathers', 'hospitals' or 'schools'. It can become a home, a ship, a castle, a lorry, a train or an aeroplane.

A child's best friends are her parents. Mothers and fathers are often very busy or away at work. Children usually spend a lot of time with their mothers but less time with their fathers. A father should play with his children whenever he can. Children learn by talking to adults.

Encourage children to discover new ways of playing games. A child will enjoy a game more if she has invented it herself. Only stop her if it is dangerous to her or to another child.

Happy, healthy children should always be playing. If a child does not want to play then is there something wrong? Is the child sick? Is she eating enough food? Is she unhappy? Find out the reason so that soon she can be playing happily again.

TIME SPENT IN PLAY IS NEVER WASTED

Father telling stories

Questions for pupils
1. Why is playing important for children?
2. How can we play with small babies? Why should we talk to them?
3. What is the purpose of a pre-school playgroup?
4. What can a child learn from playing shops?
5. Why is a doll a good toy for boys and girls?
6. How do picture books help children learn?
7. How many uses do bottle tops have?
8. What is a climbing frame made from?

Activities for pupils

Activities marked* are directed at older children and teachers
1. Draw a poster of children playing.
2. Make a doll and baby carrier for a child you know. Give the doll a name and sew or draw the name onto the baby carrier.*
3. How many things can you find in your home to make into toys?
4. Make a collection of things for children to play with in water or sand.*
5. Make some glue and glue brushes. Show some children how to make pictures with leaves, petals, sand or coloured paper.*
6. Make a collection of empty matchboxes and blocks of wood for building bricks.
7. Find an old car tyre and hang it from a tree.
8. Visit your local playgroup. Help the playgroup leader with games. If there is no playgroup write a letter to the Ministry of Education asking them where there is a course for playgroup leaders.*
9. Make some musical instruments and start a band.
10. Make a safe play area near your home or school. Build a climbing frame.*
11. Play Happy Healthy Snakes and Ladders (see p.94).

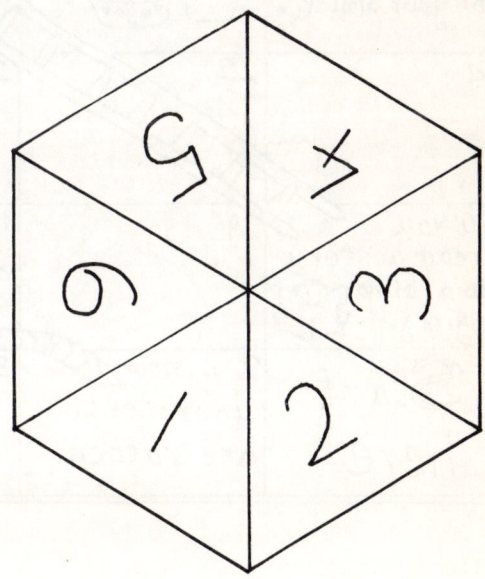

Copy this onto some card.
Push a short stick through the middle.
Spin to see how many squares you may move.
If you land at the bottom of a ladder, go UP it.
If you land on the head of a snake, do DOWN it.
Use seeds, stones or bottle tops as markets.
2, 3, 4, 5 or 6 people may play together.
The first player to reach the square 100 is the winner, but he must spin the exact number needed.

100 You have grown into a happy, healthy adult!	99	98 You only had cool-drink for lunch..	97	96
81	82 ... now you have vegetables for all the family.	83	84	85 .. now you have eggs for supper
80 You drank from a dirty stream..	79	78	77	76
61	62 ... now she is better.	63 You planted a garden...	64	65
60 .. now you have diarrhoea.	59	58	57 You build a chicken run....	56 ...now you are hungry.
41	42	43	44 ... now you will not eat germs.	45
40 You make a Special Drink for your sister..	39	38 ... now she has a friend.	37	36 You wash your hands before eating
21	22	23	24 ... now you are sick.	25
20 You read a story to a blind girl...	19	18 You ate sweets and never cleaned your teeth..	17	16 ... now you feel bright and ready to work.
1 Start here	2 ... now your teeth are rotten.	3	4 You ate peanuts and paw-paw for school lunch...	5

Happy, Healthy

	94 Your brother is bottle fed..	93	92	91
..now he is in and sick	87	88 You never washed your body...	89 ..now you have no flies in your home.	90
	74 ...now she stays well	73	72	71 ...now you have scabies.
You ate rotten food..	67	68	69 You ignore a deaf boy...	70
	54	53 You help build a ventilated latrine...	52	51 ..now it has healed well.
ur sister was munised at e clinic...	47 You swam in a river...	48	49 ..now he feels lonely.	50
	34 You ate nothing before school..	33 ..now you are big and strong.	32	31 You washed your cut foot with clean water.
..now have ilharzia.	27	28	29 ..now she has a strong healthy baby.	30
	14	13 ..now you cannot think about school work.	12	11
ou were east fed for o years..	7	8	9	10 You took your mother to ante-natal clinic...

Snakes and Ladders

10 How should children progress?

At birth babies can already do many things. They can cry, hear, see, wave their arms and legs, and suck milk from their mothers, but they do not know why they are doing these things. They do them from **instinct**. During the next few years they will learn to do things because they want to and to think about them first.

Crying is the most noticeable thing new-born babies can do. Babies cry when they are hungry, in pain, have a wet napkin or are tired. Mothers usually learn the difference between cries. Sometimes babies cry because they want to be held and talked to. Babies should be talked to as much as possible. Bathe them in words and singing.

Here is a guide to what babies can do at different ages:

3 weeks — A baby can follow things with her eyes. She sleeps a lot during the day but wakes to be fed at night.

6 weeks — She will smile at people — if they smile at her. The more you smile at a baby, the happier she will be and the more she will learn.

3 months — She holds her head up on her own. She will be taking more interest in things around her, especially faces and her own hands.

4 months — She moves her head round to look at things that interest her. She can sit up if supported. She eats soft food.

5 months — She is interested in sounds and music and she will turn her head to listen. If you hold a spoon near her she will reach out and grasp it.

6 months — She rolls over. If you hold her standing up she can support her weight on her legs.

7 months — She chews anything she can hold. She will hold her arms out to be picked up.

8 months — She sometimes becomes less friendly with strangers. She prefers her mother or other members of the family. She sits up on her own.

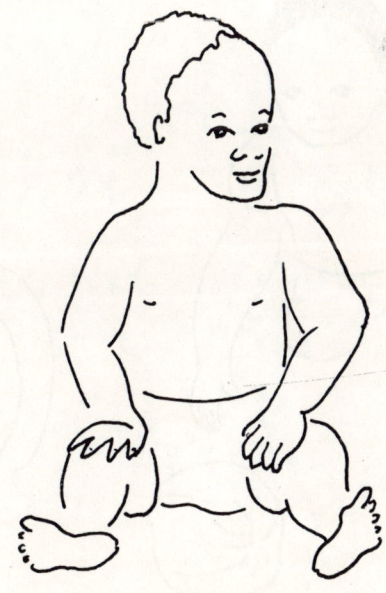

8 months

9 months	She is beginning to crawl on her hands and knees. She can also pick up small things with her fingers — and put them in her mouth!
10 months	She can drink from a cup. She pulls herself up to stand, but still has to hold on to a person or a chair. She can wave 'goodbye.'
12 months	She feeds herself with a spoon or her fingers. She can walk if one hand is held. She can clap her hands together. She is beginning to say simple words like 'mama' and 'baba'.
15 months	She can walk on her own. During the next year her talking will improve.
2 years	She can speak sentences of 2 or 3 words and knows the names of many things. She will understand what is said to her. Two-year-old children often get angry because they cannot say what they want to.
3 years	She says quite a lot. She enjoys going to pre-school playgroup and playing with other children. She can hold a pencil and draw with it. She looks at pictures in books and can name the things she sees. She can dress herself and do up big buttons. Getting undressed is more difficult. She will be toilet trained and may be dry at night.

9 months   14 months

4 years   She can talk well. She can draw simple pictures. She can brush her teeth and wash her face and hands on her own. She can bang a large nail with a hammer.

5 years   She can dress and undress herself. She can tie up shoe-laces. She can draw houses, animals and people. She is looking forward to school.

Not all babies and children progress at the same speed. Some are slow at walking but learn to talk early. Other children may walk very early but not learn to talk until nearly 3 years old. Do not worry about a child unless she is very far behind for her age. Sometimes being backward shows there is something physically wrong with her. For example, if she does not smile for many months then she may be blind or if she does not say any words by the age of 2 years then she may be deaf. Finding out these things as early as possible is important for the child's future progress. Sometimes a child is slow because she has a damaged brain. The brain cannot be mended but the child can be taught many things.

Babies all learn from other people. If babies are left on their own they will not progress. Watching babies grow up and learn new skills is always interesting. They need lots of encouragement while they are learning to fit into the world. Don't laugh *at* them if they do something wrong; laugh *with* them because they are trying.

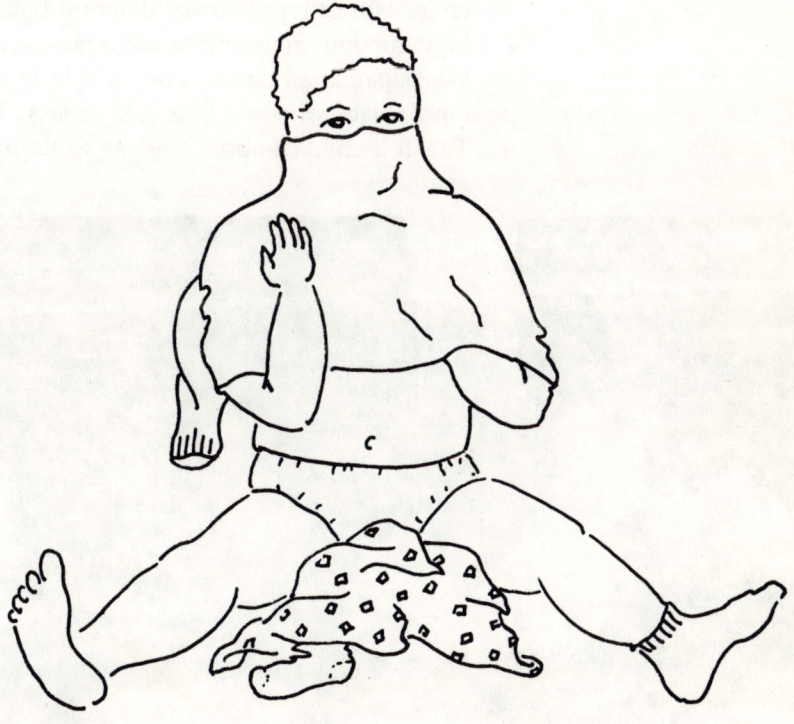

Learning to dress

Questions for pupils
1 At what age can a baby hold her head up? When can a baby sit up?
2 What is the danger of giving a baby nuts to play with?
3 What could it show if a baby cannot talk at all at 2 years? What should the mother do?
4 What can a 3 year-old child do?

Activities for pupils
1 Find a new-born baby in your village or street. Keep a chart of her age. Write on it when she learns to do new things. Compare your chart with other charts of different babies.
2 Imagine you are one year old again. Write a story about what it feels like begin small and not being able to walk or talk.
3 Find a baby of about one year or less. Teach her to clap her hands.
4 Teach a child of about 5 years to tie up shoe-laces.

11 What should children wear?

Children need clothes that are comfortable to wear, cheap to buy and easy to wash. Cotton is the best fabric. Cotton is cooler in summer and warmer in winter than other fabrics because it absorbs sweat. Man-made fabrics become sticky in both hot and cold weather.

Children grow so fast that some clothes fit them for only a few months. Certain styles of clothes 'grow' with a child and will last longer. For boys, shorts are cheaper and will fit them for longer than long trousers. Shorts with elastic waists are cheaper than shorts with belts and zips. They are also safer: many boys catch their penises in the zips of shorts or trousers. This is very painful!

Long sleeved shirts can have tucks sewn in above the elbows until the child's arms grow. For most of the year short sleeved shirts and blouses will do.

T-shirts are the most comfortable and cheap top for both boys and girls and they do not need much ironing. Ironing clothes kills the germs and the eggs of the putse fly which burrows under the skin. Ironed clothes look and feel much smarter too.

For girls, choose dresses that are not made with tight bodices or tight sleeves. Girls grow out of waisted dresses more quickly than dresses with either a high waist or no waist at all. Make sure the dress has a good hem at the bottom for letting down later. A frill of a different colour can be added to make a dress longer.

If you can sew you need only 1½ metres of fabric to make a pretty dress for a 3 to 5 year-old girl. Make it in a style that is easy for her to put on and take off on her own with no buttons or zips down the back.

If children are clean and their clothes are clean, ironed and without holes they look just as smart in everyday clothes as they do in expensive party clothes for special occasions. Lace dresses for girls and suits for boys are usually out-grown long before they are worn-out.

In the winter a child needs a warm jersey. Knitting one yourself is cheaper than buying one. Choose a pattern with simple stitches and a bright colour that will not show the dirt. A white jersey is white on a child for only a few minutes! Make sure it is big enough to last and long enough to cover the belly properly. A warm hat and scarf are easy to knit too.

A child need not wear lots of clothes just because an adult feels cold. Children who are running about and playing feel warmer than an adult

does while sitting.

Wearing wet clothes is not good for anyone. Make a raincoat out of a large plastic sack. Cut holes for the head and arms. Even a paper sack will keep someone drier than nothing.

Sleeping in nothing at night is better than wearing the clothes that have been worn all day. If it is not possible to have clean clothes every day then the clothes should be hung up at night to air them. Make a nightdress or pyjamas for wearing in bed. Hang them in the sun during the day. Blankets should be hung out in the sun to air too.

Small babies lose a lot of heat from their heads in the winter. Knit a wool hat for a baby for cold days.

Clothes need washing as often as bodies. Dirty clothes help skin infections to grow. Clean clothes look and feel nicer to wear.

Children who wear shoes cannot catch hookworms, cut their feet or get thorns in their feet. Wearing canvas shoes all the time is better than having a pair of expensive leather shoes that are only worn on special occasions.

How to make a simple dress, nightdress, pyjamas or shorts for a 4 to 6 year-old child

For the dress you will need:
1 m cotton fabric (90 cm wide) Nightdress: 1.10 metres
1 m narrow elastic
sewing thread to match fabric
needle, pins, scissors, newspaper, ruler, pencil and tape-measure

For pyjamas you will need:
1.5 m cotton fabric
60 cm narrow elastic
sewing thread to match fabric
needle, pins, scissors, newspaper, ruler, pencil and tape-measure

Dress, nightdress or pyjama top
1 Measure the child with the tape-measure.
2 With the ruler draw the shapes shown in the diagram onto some newspaper. Check that you have 2 sleeves, 1 back, 1 front and strips of fabric 4 cm wide and 1 m long. The strips can be in several pieces. For a nightdress make longer back and front pieces (see fig 1a). For pyjamas make shorter back and front pieces.

3 Cut out the newspaper pieces.
4 Hold the newspaper pieces for the back and sleeves against the child to make sure that they are the right length.
5 Lay the fabric out on the floor.
6 Pin the paper pieces onto the fabric. Arrange the pieces so there are no spaces between them. This will save fabric.
7 Cut out the pieces.
8 Place the *right sides* of the fabric together and pin. Sew the sleeves to the body along edges A — B. (see figs 1a and b)
9 Pin and sew the sleeves and body along X — A — Y, with *right* sides together.
10 Sew the strips of fabric together at the ends.
11 Sew the strips of fabric all around the neck edge, with *right* sides together. Fold the strips over and sew inside.
12 Fold up a bottom hem on the body and sew.
13 Fold up a hem along sleeve edge and sew.
14 Using a safety-pin or paper-clip, thread elastic around neck edge and sleeves.

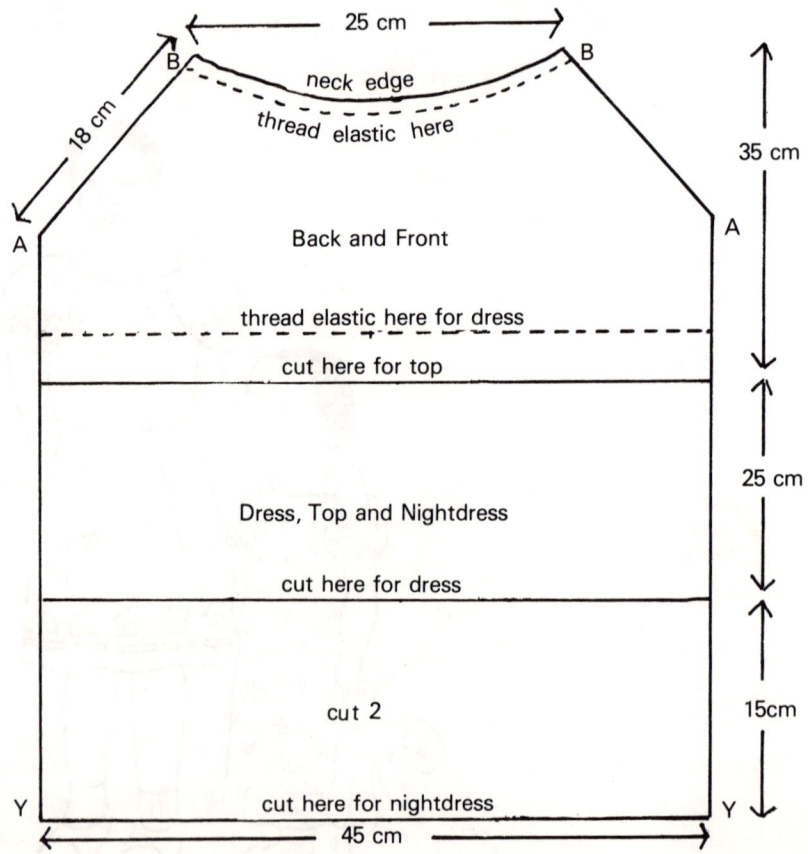

Fig 1a

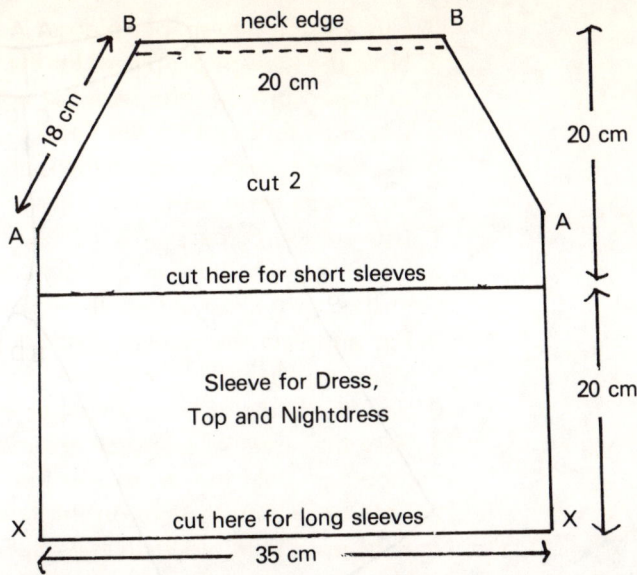

Fig 1b

Pyjama trousers or shorts

1. Measure the child to make sure the trousers will be the right length.
2. With a ruler and pencil draw the shapes onto newspaper. For shorts make the trousers shorter (see fig 2a)

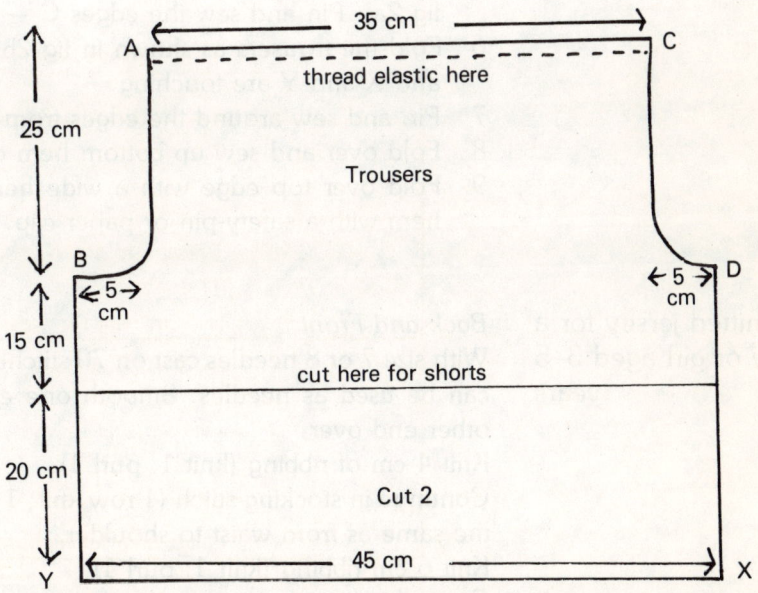

Fig 2a

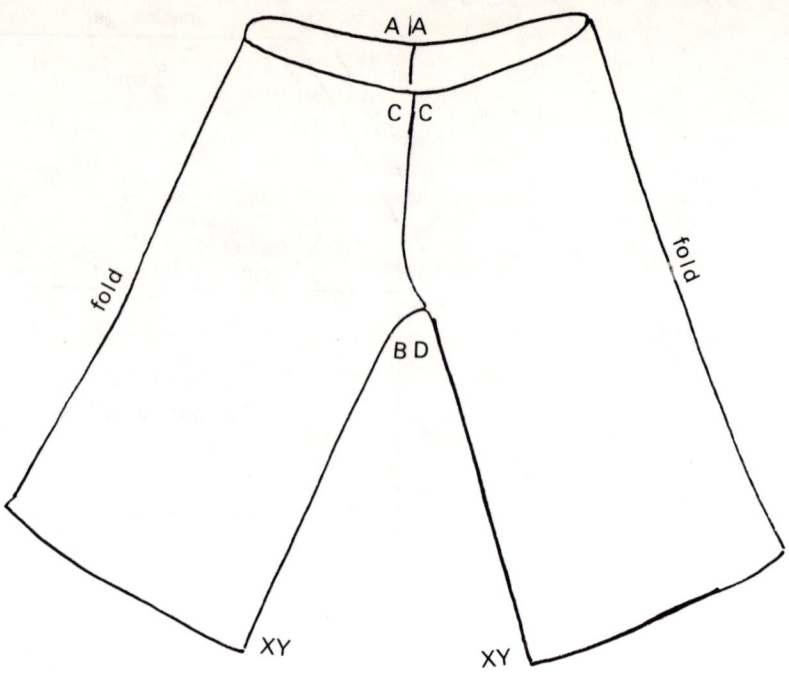

Fig 2b

3 Cut out and check the paper pieces against the child.
4 Pin the paper pieces onto the fabric and cut out.
5 Pin the *right sides* of the fabric together. Sew the edges A — B (see fig 2a). Pin and sew the edges C — D together.
6 Fold the trousers as shown in fig 2b so that B and D are touching and X and Y are touching.
7 Pin and sew around the edges from XY to DB on both legs.
8 Fold over and sew up bottom hem of trousers or shorts.
9 Fold over top edge with a wide hem. Thread elastic through the hem with a safety-pin or paper-clip.

Knitted jersey for a boy or girl aged 3–5 years

Back and Front
With size 7 or 8 needles cast on 70 stitches. Lengths of wire coat hanger can be used as needles. Smooth one end on a stone, and bend the other end over.
Knit 4 cm of ribbing (knit 1; purl 1).
Continue in stocking stitch (1 row knit; 1 row purl) until piece measures the same as from waist to shoulder.
Knit 6 cm ribbing (knit 1; purl 1).
Cast off.
Repeat for back.

Sleeves
Cast on 60 stitches. Knit 4 cm of ribbing.
Continue in stocking stitch until piece measures the same as from wrist to shoulder.
Cast off.
Repeat for second sleeve.

Sewing up
Fold each sleeve in half and sew along edge.
Sew back and front together along sides, leaving enough room at the top to insert sleeves.
Sew in sleeves.
Sew along shoulders, leaving enough space for the head.

Questions for pupils
1. What sort of clothes are best for children?
2. Why should children wear shoes?
3. Why are clean clothes better than dirty clothes?

Activities for pupils
Activities marked* are directed at older children
1. Draw a picture of children playing in comfortable clothes.
2. Write a story about a pair of shoes. Where did they go? What did they see?
3. Make a dress for a little girl you know.*
4. Make some pyjamas or shorts for a boy you know.*
5. Knit a jersey in bright colours.*

12 What is child spacing

When everyone lived in the rural areas it was important to have a large family. The children could help with the growing of food, feeding chickens, herding cattle and hoeing the fields. As each family grew, so more land could be cultivated. Children did not go to school then, so they had more time to help the family.

In the old days many more babies and children died before they became adults. Sometimes whole families of children died in a few weeks from a disease such as measles. Parents had to have many children to make sure that some of their children survived to be adults.

Today everyone's health can be improved and more children live to be adults so, if the same number of children are born, families will be bigger because more of them survive.

While a mother is breast-feeding she is less likely to become pregnant because she may not have periods, but if a baby is bottle-fed or the mother stops breast-feeding then she will soon become pregnant.

Mothers used to breast-feed their babies until they were at least 3 years old so there were a few years between each child. If a woman does not breast-feed her child and she does not use **birth control** then she could have a baby every year from when her periods start until her periods stop. This could be for 30 years!

Today more people live in towns and cities. If a family has many children they have to squeeze into the same sized house. The large family cannot grow more food to feed all their children because there is not enough land in towns and cities. Even in the rural areas all the good land is already cultivated. If parents have a lot of children there will be less land for the children to share when they grow up. If everyone keeps on having big families there will soon not be enough land or jobs for all of them. There are too many people in the rural areas for all of them to have as much land as they want.

The father will earn the same amount of money whether he has 2 or 12 children. The mother will not have time to work for money if she is busy looking after a large family. If there are fewer children in each family then there will be more food to go round and so better health. There will be more money and so better education. Well-spaced children do better at school. Their parents have more time to spend with their children.

Child spacing means having a few years between the children in the family. A mother who has a new baby every year will have less time and energy to look after the first baby. If she waits 3 or 4 years she will be able to look after each baby well. The mother can breast-feed her child until she is at least 2 years. If she wants to have another baby after that, both she and the child will be strong. Mothers who have many babies in a short time may become sick and weak. A woman's body needs a rest between babies in order to regain its strength.

Children are like maize . . .

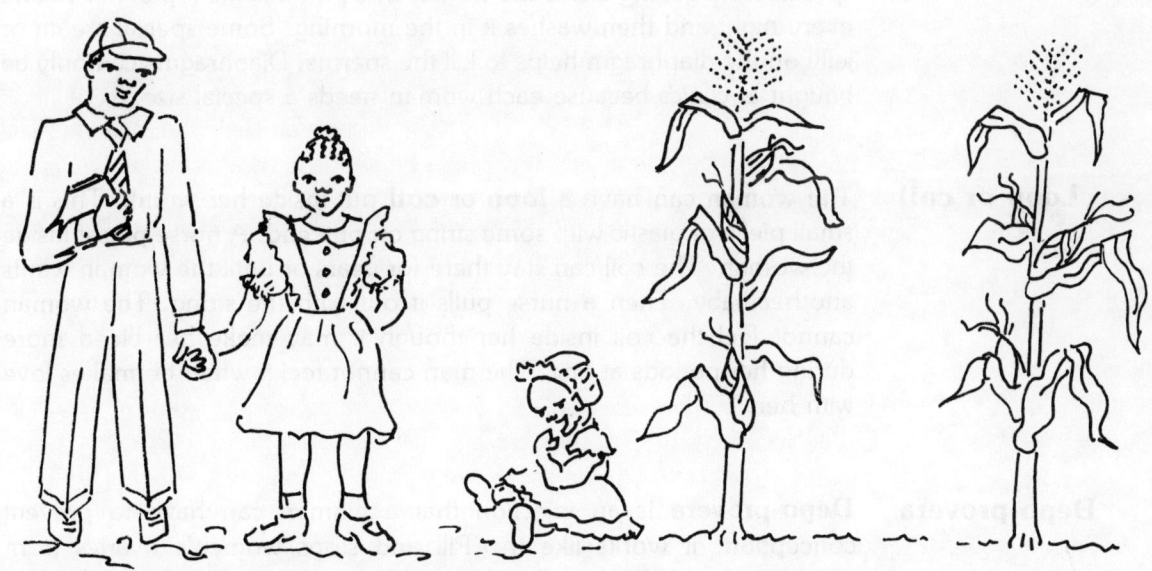

. . . they need space to grow well.

Having many babies in a short time is like growing many vegetables in a small patch of ground: all the vegetables will be small and stunted. Some of them will die because each plant will only get a small amount of food and water. If there is a big space between the vegetables they will each grow big and strong. Children are like vegetables: they need plenty of space between them. A space of 3 or 4 years between children is good. Then the parents can spend more time with each child. The child will have enough food, clothes and care. She will grow into a strong, healthy adult.

In the old days there was nothing to stop women from becoming pregnant. Now there are lots of ways to prevent babies starting. This is called child spacing or **birth control**. All the methods of birth control stop pregnancy from developing. This allows the parents to decide when they want their next baby.

Methods for child spacing

The pill The woman can take a birth control pill every day. These pills will stop her ovaries from making eggs. She will still have periods but she cannot become pregnant. She must take the pill every day. If she forgets then she may become pregnant.

Diaphragm The woman can wear a **diaphragm** inside her. This is a small rubber cap that covers the entrance to the womb. The diaphragm stops the sperms from getting inside the womb. She puts it at the top of her vagina every night and then washes it in the morning. Some special cream or jelly on the diaphragm helps to kill the sperms. Diaphragms can only be bought at clinics because each woman needs a special size.

Loop or coil The woman can have a **loop** or **coil** put inside her womb. This is a small piece of plastic with some string on one end. A nurse puts it inside the woman. The coil can stay there for years or until the woman wants another baby. Then a nurse pulls it out with the string. The woman cannot feel the coil inside her though it may make her bleed more during her periods at first. The man cannot feel it when he makes love with her.

Depo-provera **Depo-provera** is an injection that a woman can have to prevent conception. It works like the Pill and stops women's ovaries from making eggs. A Depo-provera injection is given every 3 months at a clinic. It is a good birth control method for women who might forget to take a pill every day or forget to use a diaphragm. It can prevent women from having babies for some time after it is used so most clinics only give it to women who have had all the babies they want.

Breast-feeding
While a woman is breast-feeding she might not have periods. Once her baby starts eating food and breast-feeding less often her periods will start again. She should start using birth control soon after the birth of her last baby otherwise she may get pregnant. If she does not breast-feed at all she will certainly get pregnant very quickly.

Condom or sheath The man can wear a **condom**. This is a narrow bag of thin rubber that fits over his penis and catches the sperm. The condom prevents the sperm from reaching the woman's egg. After making love the man throws it away or washes it for next time. Condoms are very cheap and can be bought in shops or clinics.

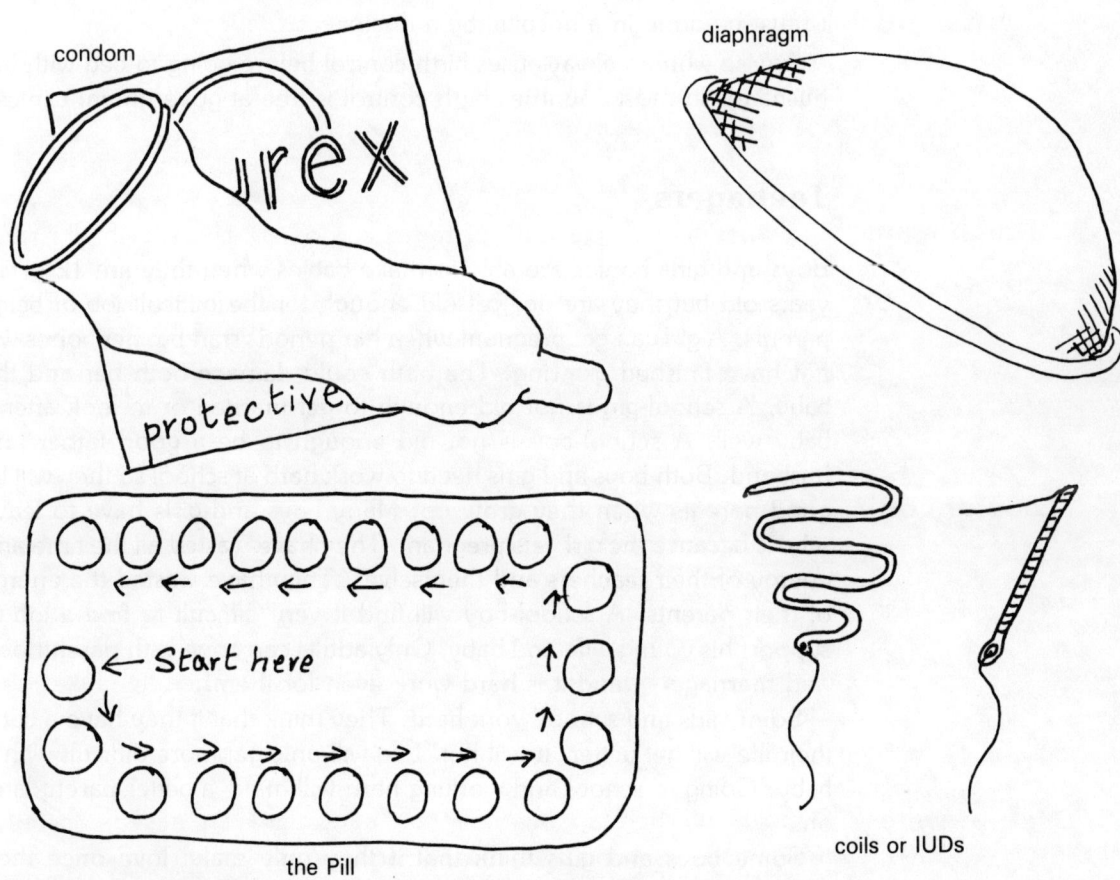

Methods for child spacing

Sterilisation If a man and woman have had all the children they want one of them can have a **sterilisation** operation. This is a small operation done in hospital. In a woman the tubes that carry the eggs from the ovary to the womb are cut and tied-up. The woman will still have periods but she cannot have any more babies. In a man the tubes that carry the sperm from his testicles (balls) to his penis are cut and tied-up. He can still enjoy making love with his wife. The semen will come out of his penis but there will be no sperms, or seeds, in it so his wife cannot get pregnant.

Abortion If a woman becomes pregnant and she does not want the baby she may try to **abort** it. This means making the unborn baby come out too early so that it dies. Abortion is very dangerous. It may kill the woman as well as the baby. Abortion is against the law in most countries and anyone who helps a woman to abort can be sent to prison. If a woman aborts she can easily become infected and have poisoned blood. This will make her very ill or even kill her. If she lives she may never be able to have any more babies when she wants to. In countries where abortion is permitted it must be done in a hospital by a doctor.

A wise woman always uses birth control before going to bed with her husband. In most countries birth control is free at government clinics.

Teenagers

Boys and girls bodies are able to make babies when they are 12 or 13 years old but they are not yet old enough for the difficult job of being parents. A girl can get pregnant when her periods start but her bones will not have finished growing. The birth could damage both her and the baby. A school-girl is not old enough to get married or to look after a baby well. A school-boy is not old enough to be a good father and husband. Both boys and girls need to work hard at school so they will be good parents when they grow up. Many boys and girls have to leave school because the girl gets pregnant. They have wasted all the time and energy of their teachers and themselves. They have wasted the energy of their parents. A school-boy will find it very difficult to find a job to support his young wife and baby. Only adults can cope with parenthood and marriage — and it is hard work even for them!

Some girls find school-work hard. They think that if they have a baby their life will get better. It will not. Life will only get more difficult with a baby. Going to school and working hard will make a better parent later on.

Some boys and girls think that if they only make love once then pregnancy cannot happen. Unless a couple are using a proper method of birth control the girl will get pregnant. Many boys say to girls, 'I will only love you if you will make love with me'. This is not true. If the boy really loves the girl then he will not insist in this way.

Boys and girls often cannot help falling in love but they must remember that strong feelings can have serious results if they are not careful. Teenagers fall in and out of love very easily. If a boy and girl think they are in love it does not mean that they must make love.

Sexually Transmitted Diseases

A **sexually transmitted disease** (STD) can be caught only by making love with someone who has the disease. A couple who only ever sleep with each other cannot catch any of the STDs but if men or women have many different partners then they may easily catch an STD and also pass it on to the next partner. The signs of STDs may not appear for several months. Women may have no signs and so not know that they have caught a serious disease. Every time they make love to a new partner they will pass on the disease.

If someones knows they have an STD they *must* tell their partner immediately. If they do not their partner will become dangerously sick or even die. The partner will soon re-infect the man or woman if not treated. Married men and women are often frightened to admit to their husbands or wives that they have caught an STD. Unless they bring or send their partner to a clinic soon then the health or even lives of *both* of them are in serious danger.

The two most common and dangerous STDs are *syphilis* and *gonorrhoea*.

Gonorrhoea The signs of gonorrhoea are an itching penis with yellow or white pus and pain or 'burning' in the penis when urinating. A woman may have an itching vagina or she may have no signs at all. She can still spread the germs to her partner.

After months or years the man or woman may go blind, be unable to have babies, be unable to pass urine or have great pain in the bones of the arms and legs.

The baby of a woman who has gonorrhoea may go blind. The germs go into the baby's eyes as she is born. Eyes should *never* be treated for soreness or infection with urine. The urine may contain gonorrhoea germs and blind the person.

Gonorrhoea is very common and can be caught again as soon as one attack has been treated.

Syphilis Syphilis has three stages. In the first stage a painless sore appears on the genitals. In a woman this may not be noticed. The sore goes away without treatment but the disease is still in the body. 2 weeks to 6 months later a rash or sores appear anywhere on the body. There may also be headaches, fever, loss of hair, sore throat and weakness. These signs also go away without treatment. Between two and twenty years after this the man or woman may go blind, deaf, be unable to have babies, go mad or have a weak heart. He or she finally dies.

A pregnant woman with syphilis may give birth to a dead, deformed or seriously sick baby.

Other STDs cause itching, pain, sores or pus in the genitals. These must always be treated at a clinic. Early treatment is very important with all STDs.

If all adults know the signs of STDs then they can be treated at a clinic. Health workers are never cross with patients who come with STDs. They will be treated kindly. People with STDs must not make love to anyone until the disease has been treated.

Careful washing of the genitals with soap and water by both men and women, before *and* after making love will help prevent the spread of STDs. Girls should be taught to wipe their bottoms after defecating from the front towards the back. Germs from the faeces may get into their vaginas if they wipe the other way. Men with foreskins must wash their penises especially carefully. Condoms help prevent the spread of germs between men and women.

Activities for pupils

These activities are directed at older pupils and teachers.
1. What is the purpose of child spacing? Talk about it in your class.
2. Plant some radish or cabbage seeds very close to each other in the soil. Plant some more further apart. Water them every day. Which plants grow best? Write about what you have done and what this tells you.
3. Find out how many children there are in each family in your community. How many years are there between children?
4. Discuss with your class the best age to get married. What qualities would you like in a husband or wife? How many children do you want?
5. Discuss with your class what you think is best: married life with children or staying single and having no children.

13 Disabled children

A disabled child is one who cannot do everything that other children can do. Some children are mildly disabled: they may be a bit deaf or cannot run well. Other children are severely disabled and may not able to do anything except lie on a bed. These are both **physical disabilities**. The children can think and talk. They just cannot *do* as much as other children. Some children have **mental disabilities**. Their brains cannot work well so they cannot think properly. Some mentally disabled children are just a bit slow. They can learn to read and write and look after themselves but they will never be very clever. Other mentally disabled children cannot do many things without help, even when they become adults. They will always need someone to look after them.

Disabled children are not at fault. Some disabilities happen before the child was born because the baby did not grow properly in the womb. Brain damage can happen while a baby is being born if the birth is difficult. The disability is not the mother's fault.

Other disabilities happen later through disease or accident. If a child catches polio he might get paralysis of his legs or arms. Polio can be prevented if babies are taken to the Children's Clinic for immunisation.

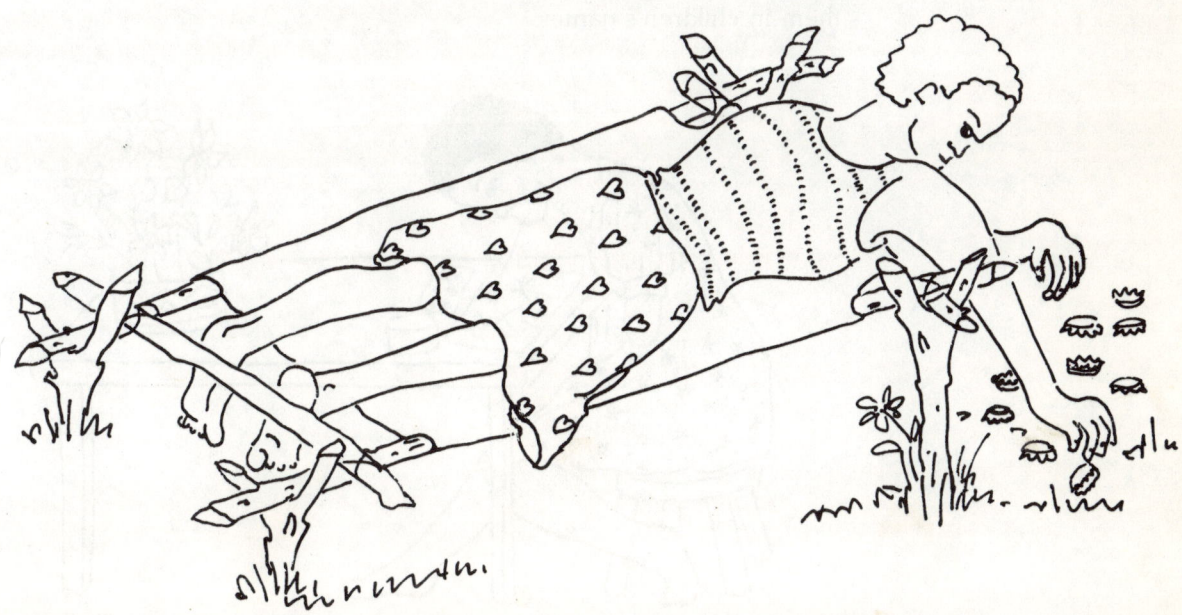

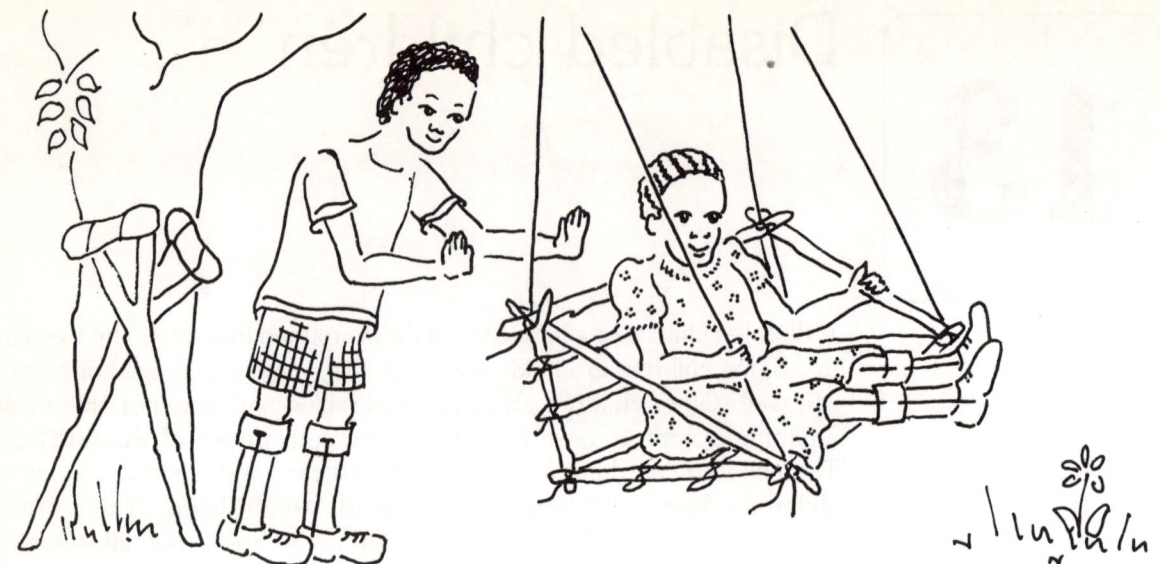

Accidents can cause disabilities. A girl may be blinded by strong acid in her eyes or a boy make break his neck falling out of a tree and never be able to walk again. Some people are disabled during war or in car accidents.

All children including the disabled have feelings. Never laugh at disabled children. Sometimes all a child can do is lie in the sun and smile; but she will only smile if there is someone to sing and talk to her. Being disabled can be very lonely. A boy who has to use crutches to walk may often be left behind when other boys run faster than him. If there are any disabled children in your village or street always include them in children's games.

Disabled children can do many things that other people can do, but it may be more difficult. There are some things they can do better than anyone else. Blind people are often very musical. A deaf child might be especially good at drawing or writing stories. A boy who uses a wheelchair may be very good at making things with his hands. If he has some carpentry tools then he can make toys or furniture. A girl who cannot use her arms and legs can write and draw with a pencil in her mouth. She might become a great artist.

LOOK FOR STRENGTHS, NOT WEAKNESSES

Blind or deaf children are not stupid. The earlier we find out if a child is deaf or cannot see well the more we can help her. Testing babies for deafness is easy. A very young baby will blink or move her head if a loud noise is made near her. If she does not show any signs of hearing then she should be taken to a clinic for more tests. When a baby can sit up she can be tested to find out how well she can hear. Sit her on the ground with someone else in front of her who can watch her movements. Stand about 1 m behind the child where she cannot see you.

Testing hearing

Rattle some seeds or nuts gently in a tin, first at one side of her and then the other side. If the baby's head or eyes do not move towards the sound then move closer. Some babies can hear loud noises but not the quiet ones. They will need extra help in learning to speak well.

A baby of only a few weeks is able to follow a moving object with her eyes. If she does not do this then she might be blind. Blind and deaf babies need to be talked to and cuddled even more than seeing and hearing babies.

An older child can be tested for deafness using a collection of objects such as a cup, a bowl and a spoon. Sit with your back to the child and quietly ask him to pass you different things.

Deaf children can be taught to speak. They will never sound quite like other people but we can still understand them. They can understand people talking by lip-reading. See if you can lip-read. Cover your ears and watch a friend speak. How much did you understand? Some deaf people use their hands for sign language.

Some signs that a child does not hear well are:
she speaks loudly;
she turns her head in one direction to hear;
she watches people's lips when they talk;
she appears rude and disobedient and
she sits apart from other children
and does not join in with their talking and games.

Blind children can learn to read with Braille books. Instead of letters, the Braille alphabet is made of raised dots that blind people can feel with their fingers.

Disabled children should not have everything done for them. If they never have to try then they will never learn. Disabled children may take longer and need more encouragement in learning a new skill. A mentally disabled boy may take five years at school before he has learnt to read and write. but it is worth it in the end. He may learn to speak English or a second language as fast and as well as any other child. Find out what a disabled child *can* do and then give encouragement.

HELP DISABLED CHILDREN TO HELP THEMSELVES

A child who cannot speak properly may be very clever. Her brain may work well but she cannot say the words. One man who could not speak or write at all made a whole book about his life. He could only make noises but his friend understood him and wrote down what he 'said'.

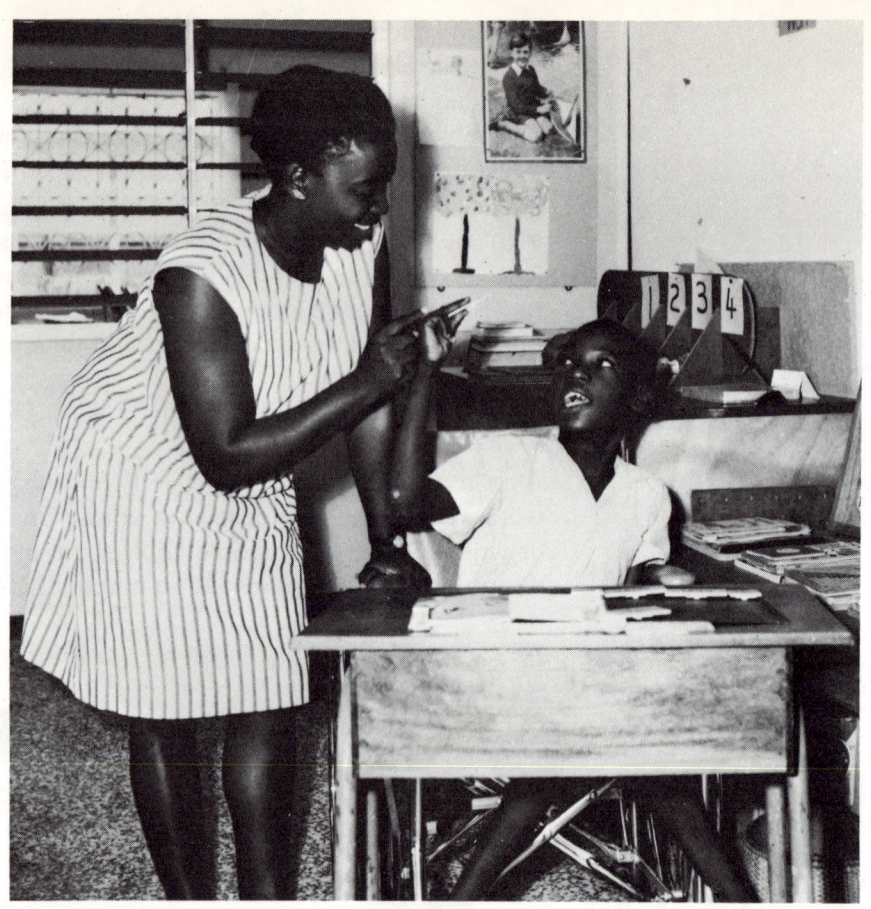

Good health care is especially important for disabled children. They need careful feeding to make sure they eat enough good food and so grow well. They must be weighed every month at the Children's Clinic and have all their immunisations. Some disabilities make children fall sick often. The local clinic should know about these children and care for them. Children who cannot move their legs may get sores on their legs and bottoms. If the child cannot feel pain the sores will get worse unless they are treated as soon as they start. A child who cannot feel pain may be given a hard bed to sleep on. This will make the sores come more often. The best bed for a child like this is made of sand. A wooden box, about 20 cm deep and big enough for the child to lie in, is filled with clean sand up to 10 cm deep. The sand will absorb sweat and urine and move to fit the shape of the body. Put a clear cotton sheet over the sand. Once a week take the top layer of sand and put it in the sun. This will kill the germs and make it fresh.

Questions for pupils

1   What is the difference between a mental disability and a physical disability?

2 Can blind people read books?
3 In what ways can people become disabled?

Activities for pupils Activities marked* are directed at older pupils and teachers.
1 Play the disabled game. One of you has a piece of wood tied to your leg so you cannot run. Another child has his eyes covered with a cloth so he cannot see. Try playing in the normal way. Take it in turns to be 'disabled'. This will show you how it feels.
2 If there is a disabled child near where you live go and visit her. Tell her stories and talk to her. Play games and cards with her.
3 If there is a disabled child near you who is over 7 years old but does not go to school, find out why. Perhaps it is because she cannot walk to school. Ask your teacher if she could come to school if you help her get there.
4 Make some simple toys for brain-damaged children: dolls; wooden cars; building bricks; a mobile.
5 Imagine you are deaf or dumb. Write a story about what it feels like.
6 Try to find your way home from school wearing a cloth over your

eyes. Take a friend with you so that you do not get run over by a car.*
7 Test all the babies and small children you know for hearing. Ask their mothers first and tell them if you think they cannot hear well.*
8 Make a sand-bed for a paralysed child.*

Making friends

Smoking, Drinking and Drugs

Smoking and drinking are two habits that many people enjoy. Neither smoking nor drinking is good for the health. Many people start drinking and smoking when they are still at school. They think it makes them look grown-up. It does not make them look grown-up; they just look foolish. Once someone starts smoking or drinking it is not easy to stop. It can be difficult to refuse if friends keep saying, 'Have another drink' or 'Have a cigarette', but they will respect someone more if he says, 'No thanks, I prefer to keep healthy' than if he is always coughing from smoking too much. They will not respect anyone who vomits all over the floor because he has drunk too much. They will not respect anyone who is always short of money because he has spent it on drink and cigarettes.

Smoking

Smoking tobacco is a habit that is not only dangerous to the health of the people who do it but also to the rest of the family. When a person breathes in cigarette smoke he is breathing in **tar** and **nicotine**. These are both poisons. Tar is a sticky substance which blocks up the **lungs**. This makes it difficult to breathe properly. The more a person smokes the more tar he will have in the lungs. This is why people who smoke always puff and pant more than others when they run. Good sportsmen and women never smoke. They want their bodies to work as well as possible.

The nicotine goes into the smoker's blood and all over the body. Nicotine prevents the heart from working well. The heart may stop for ever which will kill the smoker.

People who smoke a lot may develop and die from **lung cancer**. Lung cancer is a disease where a growth blocks up the lungs.

If a pregnant woman smokes the nicotine goes into the placenta. The baby will grow slowly and may be born small and weak. If a breast-feeding mother smokes some of the nicotine will come out in her breast-milk which the baby will drink.

One person smoking makes everyone else in the family breathe in the poisonous, smoke-filled air. A baby has very delicate lungs which can be damaged if she breathes in the smoke from cigarettes or pipes.

Smoking costs a lot of money. This money could be used for improving the family's health, rather than ruining it. For every packet of 30 cigarettes one could buy at least 12 eggs.

Drinking

Many families are unhappy and unhealthy because of **alcohol**. Drinks such as beer, lager, wine, nhipa, brandy, rum and spirits are all alcohol.

If people drink a lot of alcohol then they get 'drunk'. This stops them from thinking or working well. Studying becomes very difficult. The morning after people have drunk a lot of alcohol they will feel sick, weak and dizzy. Their bodies will ache and they may vomit.

Drunk people stop caring about their families and only care about getting more drunk. They may spend so much money on alcohol that there is none left to buy food for the children. For the price of a small bottle of beer one could buy 12 eggs or 3 loaves of bread.

A person who drinks a lot of alcohol is sick more often. In the end he or she may die from drinking. Too much alcohol causes malnutrition, mental illness, fits, loss of memory and makes a man unable to make love.

Accidents happen more often when people are drunk, especially if they are driving cars. Many accidents and deaths are caused by drunk drivers. Using machinery or tools is dangerous when people are drunk.

Drunk people often like fighting. They may hurt themselves or someone else in a fight in a beer hall or they may go home and want to fight and hurt their children.

Sometimes people drink alcohol because they want to forget about their problems; but drinking does not solve any problems. Drinking only makes problems worse. For example, a man may have many children and no work so he goes to the beer hall and gets drunk. No one will give a drunk man a job, and now he has less money to buy food for his family.

Children under 18 years old are breaking the law if they buy alcohol. If children drink alcohol they become very sick and it may damage their brains.

Drugs

Eating or smoking drugs that do not come from a clinic is very dangerous and against the law. Young people often start using drugs because their friends do. They want to be like their friends and look grown-up, but they may never become grown-up because they may die first.

People take drugs to forget about their problems and make them feel happy. Drugs are like alcohol: they do not solve any problems, they only make them worse. Drugs are even more expensive then alcohol so there is even less money left to buy food and clothes for the family.

People who take drugs do not feel hungry. They stop eating and then they become malnourished and sick. They forget about washing, so they become dirty. They forget about going to work, so there is no money. They stop caring about their families and their friends.

If children are given drugs they may either die or their bodies and brains will be damaged for ever.

Addiction **Addiction** means that a person cannot live without a certain drug. When someone starts taking drugs for fun they may find they cannot stop. Drug addicts need larger and larger amounts of the drug to satisfy them. They will do anything to get enough of the drug. They might steal, break into drug stores or even murder. If addicts do not take drugs regularly their bodies become sick and painful. This may include vomiting, diarrhoea, fits, sweating and pain lasting for over a week.

People can be addicted to drugs, alcohol or tobacco. They can be treated but the treatment takes time and patience.

Dagga Dagga is a plant that is dried and smoked, like tobacco. Users feel dreamy and sleepy and have strange thoughts. They may feel happy, giggle and forget about time or they may feel panic, be frightened, dizzy or **depressed**, lose interest in life, have headaches or vomit. This lasts a few hours but the drug stays in the body for several weeks. People who smoke dagga find learning and remembering very difficult. They cannot work well at school or college. Like cigarettes, smoking dagga damages the lungs. Users will be sick more often as the body has less strength to fight off diseases.

Driving a car or using machinery is dangerous after smoking dagga. Dagga is also called cannabis, marijuana, hashish, kif, mbanje or grass.

Pep-pills Pep-pills make the user feel unnaturally wide awake, happy and full of energy. When the effect of the drug has worn off the person feels tired, weak, hungry and depressed. People who use these drugs may develop skin sores, high blood pressure, infections or damaged brains.

LSD LSD is a drug that only affects the mind and not the body. After eating a tiny amount of LSD a person imagines strange dreams. Some people feel very calm, peaceful and forget about time. Other people may appear to go mad. They feel panic and fear, 'see' frightening things and feel depressed. These feelings usually last about a day but some people may behave strangely for many months. Sometimes people who have taken LSD think they can fly and they jump off high buildings, or they think that nothing can harm them and they walk in front of cars or trains.

Opium Several drugs are made from the opium poppy plant. Morphine and heroin are used in hospitals as pain-killers after serious accidents or operations. The drugs make people forget about pain and worry and feel happy about everything. Because this feeling is so enjoyable, people want more and more opium or heroin. Soon they cannot live without it. Addicts without heroin suffer from severe diarrhoea, vomiting, sweating, pain in the legs, back and belly for 2–10 days.

Opium is smoked like tobacco, which causes damage to the lungs. Heroin is usually injected into the blood. Heroin addicts may die from blood-poisoning because they use dirty needles. They also die from malnutrition because they forget to eat or from disease because their bodies are weakened by the drugs. Heroin is the most dangerous of all drugs.

Glue sniffing Some people breathe in the gas from glue, petrol, paraffin, paint or aerosol sprays. This makes them feel as if they are floating in air and not part of this world. When the feeling stops, they have a headache, vomit or may fall **unconscious**. Some people suffer from fear, panic, madness or want to fight others.

People who sniff glue or other poisonous liquids will damage their **kidneys**, liver, nose or mouth. Glue sniffers may die if they breathe vomit into the lungs when they are unconscious or from damage to the heart and lungs.

Questions for older pupils
1. Why is smoking bad for health?
2. What happens to a family if the parents drink a lot?
3. How many types of alcohol can you think of?
4. Why are drugs so dangerous?
5. What happens to someone who is a drug addict?
6. Where does opium come from?

Activities for older pupils
1. Draw a poster about smoking. Stick it up in your village or street.
2. Discuss in your class how you could discourage young people from smoking.
3. Write a story about a man who is always drunk. What happens to his family?
4. Discuss how drunken driving could be prevented.
5. Find out how much a packet of 20 cigarettes costs. If a man smokes 25 a day, how much will he spend in a year? How many sacks of rice or maize could he buy with the money?

6 Find someone who smokes cigarettes. What colour are the teeth and fingers? Ask the person to breathe cigarette smoke through a white handkerchief or cloth. What happens? Imagine what the insides of this person's lungs look like after hundreds of cigarettes.
7 Have a discussion with your class about good health habits and bad health habits. How could you help to make your country a healthier place?

Glossary:

meanings of words, in alphabetical order

Abortion	when a baby in the womb is destroyed or born before it is formed, so that it dies.
Alcohol	drink that affects the mind and body.
Anaemia	when the blood is poor. The signs are tiredness, pale gums and eyelids and no energy.
Ante-natal	clinic for pregnant women.
Anti-bodies	very small particles in the blood which help fight disease.
Asbestos	a rock that causes disease if small amounts of dust from it are breathed in.
Aspirin	tablets which help headaches, fever and body pains. Can be bought in most shops.
Balanced meals	meals with a good mixture of food.
Bilharzia	a worm disease of the bladder and belly. It is caught in rivers and streams and damages many parts of the body.
Birth control	prevention of pregnancy. Allows the parents to choose when they want to have children.
Bladder	the bag in the belly which holds urine.
Blair pit latrine	a latrine that has no flies and does not smell.
Blister	liquid under a 'bubble' of skin.
Bronchitis	disease of the lungs. Signs are fever, coughing and pain in lungs.
Calamine lotion	a pink cream that stops skin itching. It does *not* cure scabies, ringworm or skin infections.
Cancer	a lump that grows in the body usually until it is either cut out or the person dies.
Cells	the body is made from millions of cells. Bodies are built of cells as houses are built of bricks.
Child spacing	having a few years between the children in the family.
Chloroquine	a drug to prevent and treat malaria.
Coil	small piece of plastic that fits in the woman's womb to prevent pregnancy (a type of birth control).
Cold	a common disease easily caught from other people.
Conception	when a male sperm and the female egg join together inside the woman's body.
Condom	narrow rubber bag which fits over a man's penis to prevent pregnancy (a

	type of birth control).
Crutches	sticks to help a lame person walk.
Defecate	discharge faeces from the body.
Deformed	not grown properly.
Dehydration	loss of water from the body. Prevent with Special Rehydration drink.
Dentist	health worker who looks after teeth.
Depo-provera	three monthly injection given to women to prevent pregnancy (a type of birth control).
Depression	feeling very unhappy.
Diarrhoea	runny or liquid faeces.
Diaphragm	a shallow rubber cap that fits over the opening to a woman's womb to prevent pregnancy (a type of birth control).
Diptheria	a serious disease of the throat. Prevent with immunisation.
Energy food	food that gives the body energy and helps it to grow.
Exhaustion	extreme tiredness.
Faeces	waste which leaves the body through the anus.
Fertilisation	same as conception.
Fertiliser	chemicals to make crops grow well.
Fever	when the body becomes very hot because of disease.
Fits	sudden unnatural movement of the body and unconsciousness.
Flu	disease like a bad cold. May cause vomiting and diarrhoea as well as fever and aching body.
Foetus	the unborn baby.
Gentian violet	purple liquid that kills germs on the skin.
Germ	the very small living things that cause disease. They are so small we cannot see them.
Germ-free	anything that is so clean that there are no germs on it.
Giddiness	a feeling that everything is going round.
Genitals	the penis and scrotum in a man; the vagina in a woman.
Gonorrhoea	a sexually transmitted disease.
Growing food	food that makes the body grow and stay healthy.
Gut	part of the belly where food is broken down.
Immunisation	injection which prevents dangerous disease by making anti-bodies in the blood.
Immunity	an ability to fight off certain diseases.
Impetigo	a skin infection usually of the face.
Infection	many germs growing in or on the body.
Instinct	things people do without being taught. Sucking, chewing and smiling are instincts.
Iodine	Found in small amounts in some foods. Very small amounts are needed in our food to prevent disease.

Jaundice	a disease that makes the eyes and skin go yellow.
Kidneys	two organs in the belly which filter urine.
Kiss of Life	breathing into the mouth of an unconscious person who has stopped breathing to make him breathe again.
Kwashiorkor	a disease of malnutrition.
Larvae	young worm-like animals that come from the eggs of insects. For example, mosquitoes and bilharzia.
Latrine	a hole or pit in the ground that is used as a toilet.
Liver	an organ in the belly which filters blood. The liver of cows, chickens, sheep, pigs or fish is very good food.
Loop	see **coil**.
Lungs	the part of the body that we breathe with. There are two above the belly.
Malaria	a disease carried by mosquitoes. It causes fever, anaemia and bad headaches.
Malnourished	a person who does not eat enough good food. A malnourished child is thin, weak, sick and has no energy.
Measles	a dangerous disease like very bad 'flu. Malnourished children may die from measles. Prevent it with immunisation.
Mental disability	when a child or adult has a damaged brain.
Midwife	a woman who helps a mother to have her baby.
Mobile	a hanging toy that moves slowly round.
Mucus	the liquid in the nose, mouth and lungs.
Mumps	a disease that makes the neck swell for a few days.
Navel	the place in the middle of the belly where the umbilical cord was attached.
Nicotine	poison in cigarette smoke.
Ovary	two organs in the belly of the woman where eggs are made.
Paralysis	not being able to move a part of the body.
Penis	the man's sex organ.
Period	the monthly bleeding in women.
Pill, The	birth control pill which prevents pregnancy.
Placenta	part in a woman's womb at the end of the umbilical cord. It filters the blood going to the foetus.
Physical disability	when a person cannot use all the parts of his body.
Playgroup	a place for children under 7 years to play together in the care of an adult.
Pneumonia	a disease of the lungs. Causes fever, pain and sometimes death if not treated.
Poison	anything that when swallowed or breathed in makes a person sick or die.

Polio	a serious disease which can cause paralysis. Can be prevented with immunisation.
Puberty	the age when boys and girls become adults.
Pus	the yellow or white liquid made by infections. It is full of germs.
Rabies	a dangerous disease caught from the bite of infected dogs and wild pigs. It causes animals to go mad and bite people. If not treated quickly the people die very painfully. Dogs can be immunised against rabies.
Rehydration	giving water or Special Rehydration Drink to someone with diarrhoea.
Ringworm	disease of the skin, especially in children who do not wash.
Road to Health Card	card showing a baby's weight and immunisations. It is given to mothers at the children's clinic.
Sanitation	keeping public places and water clean.
Scabies	a skin disease caused by tiny animals that tunnel in the skin.
Scrotum	the bag behind a man's penis which holds the testes where the sperm are made.
Semen	the white liquid that carries a man's sperm through his penis and into a woman's womb.
Sexually Transmitted Disease	a disease caught from a sexual partner.
Sewage	water, faeces and urine collected from a town.
Shock	when someone has had an accident they become cold and sweaty.
Special Drink	sugar, salt and water mixed to prevent and cure dehydration
Sperm	the man's seeds.
Sterilisation	a simple operation for a man or woman to prevent pregnancy
Syphillis	a sexually transmitted disease.
Tar	poison found in cigarette smoke. Tar blocks up the lungs.
Testes	the balls in a man's scrotum.
Tetanus	a serious disease which kills new born babies if their umbilical cords get germs in them. Tetanus kills children and adults with dirty wounds. Tetanus can be prevented with immunisations.
Ticks	small insects that bury their heads under the skin and suck blood.
Transmitted	passed on to someone else.
Tuberculosis	(TB) a serious disease that usually affects the lungs. Can be prevented with immunisations.
Umbilical cord	the tube carrying blood and air to the foetus.
Unconscious	when someone appears to be asleep, but cannot be woken up.
Urine	the yellow liquid that comes out of the body. Piss.
Vagina	the tube from between a woman's legs to the womb. It is very soft and stretchy.
Vandal	someone who breaks things for no reason.
Vomit	food coming from the stomach through the mouth.

Whooping cough   a dangerous disease that can kill babies or damage their lungs. Can be prevented with immunisations.
Womb   the muscular bag in a woman's belly where babies are made.
Worms   small animals that get into the body and make a person weak and sick.

Bibliography

Aarons & Hawes (1979) *CHILD-to-child*, Macmillan
Ebrahim (1978) *Child Care in the Tropics,* Macmillan
Ebrahim (1978) *Practical Mother and Child Health in Developing Countries*, Macmillan
Hampton (Ed.) (1981-83) *Utano we Manicaland*, Manicaland Health Authority
CHILD-to-child leaflets, TALC
King (1972) *Nutrition for Developing Countries*, Oxford
King, King & Martodipoero (1978) *Primary Child Care*, Oxford
Morley (1979) *See How They Grow*, Macmillan
Morley (1973) *Paediatric Priorities in the Developing World*, Butterworth
Werner (1977) *Where There Is No Doctor*, Macmillan
Werner & Bower (1982) *Helping Health Workers Learn*, Hesperian
Ritchie (1983) *Nutrition and Families*, Macmillan Press Ltd

A NOTE ON THE CHILD-TO-CHILD PROGRAMME REFERRED TO ABOVE

CHILD-to-child is an international programme for teaching and encouraging school-children to concern themselves with the health of their younger brothers and sisters, or other younger children in their community. It arises out of ideas from Professor David Morley and his colleagues at the Institute of Child Health in London and has been further developed by many other people from all over the world. The programme includes simple preventive and curative activities appropriate to the local situation, which will usually be demonstrated and taught to the children in school for them to pass on within the family in the village or urban environment. However, there are no hard and fast rules and it is hoped that those concerned with the health of children and the community will design their own CHILD-to-child activities appropriate to local needs and suitable for older children to teach younger children. The programme was one of the projects of the International Year of the Child (1979).

Index

A

abortion, 112
accidents
   and disabilities, 116
   and drink, 124
   in the home, 69-72
   outside the home, 73-6
after-birth, 8
air, fresh, 51
alcohol, 124
anaemia, 7, 61
   and worms, 61, 62
animals
   on roads, 73-4
   in school, 41
   spreading of germs by, 45
ante-natal clinic, 9-11
anti-bodies, 16
ants, 29
anus, 62
apples, 32
apricots, 32
asbestos, 51
asprin, dosage of, 59
avocado pears, 29, 32, 37

B

babies
   deformed, 9
   playing with, 80
   and smoking, 123-4
baby carrier, doll's, how to make, 83
baby foods, home-made, 37
baby oil, 64
'bad' milk, 18
balanced diet, 33, 34-5, 40

balancing, 87
balls, 88
banana stems, as water pipes, 88
bananas, 29, 37
bandages, 76
bathing, 47
   of babies, 22, 80
beans, 29, 31, 32
bed, for disabled child, 120
bilharzia, 65
birth, 12-13
birth control, 108-12
blackcurrants, 32
bladder, 65
Blair pit latrine, 50
bleach, poisoning by, 70
bleeding (period), 6, 7
blindness, 99
   and measles, 66
   and S T D, 113
blisters, during chicken-pox, 63
blood, 53
   in urine, 65
blow football, 88
books, 86
bottle tops, 86
bottle-feeding, 17, 19-20
Braille, 119
bread, 29, 31
breast-feeding, 16-19, 28
   and birth control, 111
   and child spacing, 108
   and sick babies, 56
breasts, during pregnancy, 11
breathing
   difficult, 53
   making easier, 60
broken bones, 75
bronchitis, 59
brushing, of teeth, 48-9
burns, 69-70
buttons, 98, 101

C

cabbage, 32, 37
calamine lotion, 63, 64
cancer of the lung, 123
cannabis, 125
car accident, 75
carrots, 32
cassava, 29
cattle, on roads, 74
cereals, 32, 33
cheese, 31
chickenpox, 63
CHILD-to-child programme, 137
child spacing, 108-12
chloroquine, 64-5
choking, 72
cigarettes, poisoning by, 70
clay, for modelling, 85
cleanliness
   of clothes, 102
   and disease prevention, 1-2
   of feeding bottle, 19
   and germs, 44-5
climbing frame, making a, 90
clinic, children's, 23-6
clinic, playing at, 81-2
clothes, 4
   for babies, 21
   for children, 101-7
   for pregnant women, 11
clothing, excess of, and fever, 58
coffee, 34
coil, 110
colds, 59
conception, 7-8
condom, 111
cooking fat, 29
cooking fire, 69
cotton, for babies, 21
cotton, for clothing, 101
cough medicine, 59

coughs, 26, 59-60
counting, 86
cow meat, causing tapeworms, 61
crying, 14-15, 96
cuts, 76
    and tetanus, 66-7
cycling, 74-5

D

dagga, 125
deafness, 99
    testing for, 117-8
deformed babies, 9
dehydration, 56-7
dentist, 48
Depo-provera, 110-11
detergents, poisoning by, 70
diaphragm, 110
diarrhoea, 18, 56-8, 26
    and bottle-feeding, 19
    and germs, 45
    and measles, 66
    and worms, 62
diphtheria, 24, 25, 67
disabled children, 115-20
disease, and young babies, 16
diseases, sexually transmitted, (STD), 113-4
dog bites, 73
dogs, behaviour of on roads, 73-4
dolls, 82-3
doll's baby carrier, how to make, 83
dress, how to make, 103-4
dresses, 101
drinking, 123, 124
    during pregnancy, 8
drowning, 76
drugs, 124-6
    during pregnancy, 9

E

eating
    and disease, 1-2
    painful, 61
    during sickness, 55-6
egg (human), 6, 7, 8
eggs, 31, 32
electric shock, 72

energy foods, 29-30, 54
eyes, yellow, in babies, 18

F

faeces, 45, 46
    and worms, 61-2
fainting, 77
families, with many children, 108
father
    and child's play, 92
    and birth, 12
feeding, of babies, 16-21
feelings, 2-4
female babies, 7
fertilisation, 7
fertilisers, in river water, 49
fever, 26, 53, 54, 58-9
    during chickenpox, 63
    with coughs, 60
    and malaria, 64
    from ticks, 63
fingernails, 47
fire, in the home, 69
fish, 31, 32
fits, 58
flies, 46
    and latrines, 50
    and rubbish, 51
flu, 59
foetus, 8
food
    for anaemic people, 62
    for breast-feeding mothers, 17
    for energy, 29-30, 54
    for growing, 31-2
    for pregnant women, 11
    for protection against disease, 32
    see also non-foods
football, making a, 88

G

games, 81-92
garden, making your own, 41-2
gentian violet, 63, 64
germs, 44-5
    in water, 47, 49
giddiness, and worms, 62

glue, making of, 85
glue sniffing, 126
goats, on roads, 74
gonorrhoea, 113
grass, 125
    and malaria, 64
    and snakes, 73
ground-nut butter, 29
ground-nut oil, 29
ground-nuts, 31, 32, 33
growing foods, 31-2
guava, 32
guineaworm, 62-3

H

hair, at puberty, 6, 7
happiness, 2-3
hashish, 125
headaches, and malaria, 64
health care, for the disabled, 120
helping, treated as a game, 84
herbs, 32, 34
heroin, 126
high-energy foods
    and measles, 66
    during sickness, 56
highway code, 74
hookworms, 62

I

immunisation, 23-5
    against diptheria, 67
    against measles, 66
    against polio, 66
    against TB, 68
    against tetanus, 67
    against whooping cough, 61
immunity, to malaria, 64
impetigo, 64
infections, 26
insects, 31
instinct, 96
iodine, 34
itching,
    and STD, 113
    and scabies, 63
    of the anus, 62

J

jaundice, 18
jersey, knitting a, 106-7
jerseys, 101

K

kale, 32
kidney beans, 31
kidneys, 34
    damage to, and drugs, 126
kif, 125
kiss of life, 76
knitting, 101, 102, 106-7
kwashiorkor, 38, 40

L

LSD, 125-6
labour, 12
lard, 29
latrine, 45, 50
laxative, 62
lemons, 32
lights, on cycles, 75
lip-reading, 118
liver, as a food, 32
loop, 110
love, 4, 113
    for baby, 14-15
lung cancer, 123
lungs, diseases of, 59, 60,
    68, 123
lungs, and smoking, 123

M

maize, 29, 32
making love, 7
malaria, 54, 64-5
male babies, 7
malnourishment, *see* malnutrition
malnutrition, 18, 38, 40
    and bottle feeding, 19
    and drink, 124
    and drugs, 125, 126
    and tetanus, 66-7

mangoes, 32
margarine, 29
marijuana, 125
marriage, of teenagers, 112
matches, 70
    poisoning by, 70
mbanje, 125
measles, 24, 25, 55, 66
measuring strip, 38-9
meat, 31, 32
medicine bottles, dangers of, 82
medicines
    during pregnancy, 9
    poisoning by, 70
mental disability, 115
midwife, 11
milk, 31, 32
    mother's, 11
    sour, 31
millet, 31
mobile, for babies, 80
modelling, with clay, 85
morphine, 126
mosquitoes, 51, 64
mother, and child's play, 92
mouth, spots inside, 66
mucus, 60
mulberries, 32
mumps, 61
music, 89
musical instruments, making of, 89

N

napkins, 21-2
navel, 8, 13
nicotine, 123
nightdress, how to make, 103-4
non-foods, 34
nuts, 29, 31, 32

O

oil, cooking, 36
oils, 29
onions, 32
opium, 126
oranges, 32
ovary, 7

P

paint, making of, 85
palm oil, 29
paraffin, poisoning by, 70
paralysis, due to polio, 66
parents,
    and child's play, 92
    imitation of, 1
paw-paw, 32, 37
    stems, as water pipes, 88
    worm mixture, 62
peaches, 32
peanuts, 32
peas, 29, 31, 32, 37
penis, 7
pep-pills, 125
peppers, 32
period (bleeding), 6, 7, 16
petrol, poisoning by, 70
petroleum jelly, 64
pictures
    looking at, 85-6
    making of, 85
pig meat, 46
    causing tapeworms, 61
pill, the (for birth control), 110
pineapples, 32
placenta, 8, 13
plantains, 29
plastic bags, 51
play area, making a, 89-90
play, neccessity of, 79
playgroup, 81
playhouse, 91
pneumonia, 59, 60
    and measles, 66
poison, 70
polio, 24, 25, 66, 115
porridge, 29
potatoes, 29, 32, 37
pregnancy, 8-11
    and smoking, 123
problems, and drugs, 124, 125
progress, of a baby, 97-9
protective foods, 32
puberty, 6-7
pulses, 33
pumpkin, 32, 37
    seeds, 29
pus, 16
putse fly, 101
pyjamas, making a pair of, 103-6

R

rabies, 73
rag doll, how to make, 82-3
raincoat, making a, 102
rape, 32
rapoko, 29
reading, and picture books, 86
rehydration drink, 57-8
rice, 29, 31
ringworm, 63
Road to Health card, 23, 25
roads, use of, 73-5
roundworms, 62
rubbish, 46-7, 51-2

S

STD (sexually transmitted diseases), 113-4
sadness, 2-3
salt, 34
sanitation, 49
scabies, 63
school-children, and food, 37
schools, and gardens, 41-2
security, 4, 14-15, *see also* love
semen, 7
sesame seeds, 29
sewage, 49
sex, of a baby, 7
shadow play, 88
shape, learning about, 86-7
sheath, 111
sheep, on roads, 74
shellfish, 31
shining foods, *see* protective foods
shirts, 101
shock, 77
shoes, 102
shops, playing at, 81
shorts
   for boys, 101
   making a pair of, 105-6
sick babies, and breast-feeding, 56
sickness,
   signs of, 53
   see also disease
sight, test for, 118
sign language, 118
singing, 89
sitting up, by a baby, 97, 98
size, learning about, 86-7

skin diseases, 63-4
sleep, 2, 15
smoke, 51
smoking, 60, 123-4
   during pregnancy, 8-9
snails, 31
snakes, 73
solid food, introduction of, 36
sores
   and disabled children, 120
   and STD, 113-4
   caused by scabies, 63
sorghum, 29, 31
soya beans, 31
Special Rehydration Drink, 22, 57-8
speech, of a baby, 98
sperm, 7
spinach, 32
spitting, 47
spoon-feeding, 20
springs, 49
sterilisation, 112
stories, telling of to children, 86
streams, and worms, 62
sugar cane, 29
sun, playing with, 88
sunflower seeds, 29
sweet drinks, 34
sweet potato, 32, 37
sweets, 34
swing, making a, 90
syphilis, 113-4

T

TB, 24, 25, 68
talents, of the disabled, 116-7
talking,
   of a baby, 98
   to a baby, 96
tapeworms, 61
tar, 123
tea, 34
teenagers, problems of, 112-3
teeth, 48
tests
   for deafness, 117-8
   for sight, 118
tetanus, 9, 13, 24, 25, 66-7
thirst, 56
threading, 86
threadworms, 61-2

tick bite fever, 63
ticks, 63
tomatoes, 32
toothbrush, 48-9
toothpaste, 49
toys, 84-5
   for babies, 80
trousers, 101
T-shirts, 101
tuberculosis, 24, 25, 68
twins, 9-10
   and breast-feeding, 18-19

U

umbilical cord, 8, 13
   infection of, and tetanus, 67
urine
   blood in, 65
   and eye infection, 113

V

vagina, 6
vegetables, new types, 41
vomiting, 58
   in babies, 18
   and drink, 123, 124
   and worms, 62

W

walking,
   by a baby, 98
   on roads, 73-4
washing,
   of clothes, 102
   of genitals, 114
   and skin problems, 63-4
water, 49
   clean, 47
   in diarrhoea, 56-7
   playing with, 88
   and worms, 62
watercress, 32
water-holes, 49
wells, 49
wells, and worms, 62
whooping cough, 24, 25, 60-1
wires, frayed, and electric shock, 72

womb, 6
    during labour, 12
    lining of, 7
worm mixture, 62
worms, 61-3, 85
wounds, 76
    and tetanus, 66-7

Y

yams, 29
yellow eyes, in babies, 18
yoghurt, 31